WITHDRAWN FROM
TSC LIBRARY

D1447064

WITHDRAWN FROM
TSC LIBRARY

A

YANKEE IN A
CONFEDERATE TOWN

YANKEE IN A
CONFEDERATE TOWN

The journal of Calvin L. Robinson

edited by Anne Robinson Clancy

Pineapple Press, Inc.
Sarasota, Florida

Copyright © 2002 by Anne Robinson Clancy

All rights reserved. No part of this book may be reproduced in any form or by any means, electronic or mechanical, including photocopying, recording, or by any information storage and retrieval system, without permission in writing from the publisher.

Inquiries should be addressed to:

Pineapple Press, Inc.
P.O. Box 3889
Sarasota, Florida 34230
www.pineapplepress.com

LIBRARY OF CONGRESS CATALOGING-IN-PUBLICATION DATA

Robinson, Calvin L.
    A Yankee in a Confederate town / Calvin L. Robinson ; edited by Anne Robinson Woodward Clancy.— 1st ed.
cm.
    Includes bibliographical references.
    ISBN 1-56164-267-3
Robinson, Calvin L.—Diaries. 2. Jacksonville (Fla.)—History—19th century. 3.
Fernandina (Fla.)—History—19th century. 4. Florida—History—Civil War,
1861-1865—Personal narratives. 5. United States—History—Civil War,
1861-1865—Personal narratives. 6. Businessmen—Florida—Jacksonville—
Diaries. 7.Jacksonville (Fla.)—Biography. 8. Florida—History—Civil War, 1861-
1865—Social Aspects. 9. United States—History—Civil War, 1861-1865—
Social aspects. I. Clancy, Anne Robinson Woodward, 1930- II. Title.

F319.J1 R63 2002
973.7'82—dc21
[B]

                                                                        2002029307

First Edition
10 9 8 7 6 5 4 3 2 1

Design by Shé Sicks
Printed in the United States of America

Table of Contents

Foreword

The Civil War and the years immediately following were some of the worst years the American South ever endured, but we see clearly in Calvin Robinson's words that Northern and Southern sympathizers in Jacksonville, Florida, shared the pain and hardships of such an uncivil time. We discover that terrorism against Unionists was very much a part of the town Confederates' way of doing business, and we also learn that occupying Union troops burnt the town upon leaving, thereby causing much suffering among the African Americans and the other poor members of society. In a time of war, some people who might otherwise be law-abiding citizens might turn vicious and cruel. Is it the war or is it a true reflection of their lack of character? Perhaps we will never know; we can only pray that we will be spared those tragic times that test us so severely.

Robinson, a native of Vermont, had the misfortune of being in the wrong place at the wrong time. He was that Yankee in a Confederate town, and his background and his loyalty to the "old flag" affected everything in his relationship with the largely Southern population of Jacksonville. As politics polarized the community and as Robinson's relationship with the town's residents deteriorated, his very life was at stake as well as that of his family. Part of what made life especially bad for him was his standing as one of the most important merchants in town. Here was a college-educated person with power and civic standing. Had he been a person with little wealth and influence and had he kept a low profile, he may have ridden out the war with his Unionist persuasions with few major problems. This was a time, however, when almost everyone in the country espoused a position, and positions on something as gigantic as the war clearly divided the country. If you were against the majority's thinking, either Northern or Southern, you probably had a difficult time justifying your position. It was a mentality of "either you're with us or you're against us," and this is exactly where Calvin Robinson found himself—against the majority of his community and firmly convinced in the rightness of his position.

As these pages unfold, the reader will discover a personal side of the Civil War that is often lacking in history books. We need these personal experiences to help with our understanding of the time. Calvin's fears for his life are very real and his beliefs in the Union are so strong that we come away with a healthy respect for those who lived during those turbulent times and stood by their convictions. One wonders what life would have been had the Confederacy succeeded. This account from Robinson shows clearly that terrorism for political ends would have likely been the norm at least in parts of a victorious Confederacy. He writes of the local Southern sympathizers, "These men were some half dozen of the so-called southern chivalry, such as were found in every community in the South in those days—scions of broken down southern aristocracy who had squandered their patrimony, who while they still laid claim to quality, underneath a thin surface of the gentleman were— simply brutal barbarians." These are harsh words, but he called them as he saw them.

Thankfully those days of strife between North and South are gone. It took a deadly war to save the Union and to preserve for us a country of freedom and liberty. No matter which side our ancestors took, we, their descendants, are one nation again. To read about the problems of those people caught up in the events of that war is to live them vicariously, and in so doing, perhaps we can better understand where we have come from and who we are.

Thomas H. Gunn
Director of the Library
Jacksonville University
May, 2002

Acknowledgments

The past two years have been my labor of love for *A Yankee in a Confederate Town.* This volume belongs to those who search to understand our nation's past, who desire to know the experiences surrounding the historical "facts." The truth in history lies in the words and lives of men such as Calvin L. Robinson.

Many people have been instrumental in my work with the papers left by my great-grandfather, Calvin Louis Robinson. Just when I thought that the task of editing them had become three steps beyond impossible, I'd get a phone call or a long letter, and my fatigue would disappear.

Four people have literally been lifesavers. They are Thomas H. Gunn, director of the Swisher Library, and Anna Large, researcher, both from Jacksonville University; James Cusick, University of Florida, Gainesville; Robert Cornwell, computer expert; and my "new" cousin, Vivian A. Clark, of Jacksonville.

Here in Nevada, several souls provided vital encouragement: Dr. Ursula Carlson and Marilee Swirczek, Western Nevada Community College; and Wendell Huffman, Carson City Library.

But most of all, I thank my beloved son, Andrew, for his hours of proofing and his loving tolerance of numerous frozen dinners.

INTRODUCTION

$\mathcal{B}$efore his death in 1950, my father put a specific bequest in his will without sharing a word with me. He left me the awkwardly heavy package of his grandfather's memoirs. For some reason, I did not open it, but lugged my sealed burden through many moves all over the Eastern Seaboard, and finally to Nevada. I kept saying that when I retired, I would open it up and see what exactly was inside . . . but that was a long time in coming. The deep file drawer where I had stuffed the manuscript became its resting place for nearly fifty years.

Finally I opened the outer wrapping, where my mother had long ago scribbled that it contained a diary of my paternal great-grandfather's experiences during the Civil War. Inside I found 120 pages covered with minute, old-fashioned handwriting in pen and pencil on several different types of paper stock. The papers were held together in groups by handmade steel pins. Some sheets crumbled around the corners with age, and others were so faded they were barely legible. Other pages had been heavily edited with the additions rewritten on top of the old passages. My ancestor Calvin L. Robinson had worked on this memoir over an indeterminate period of time, starting in 1864.

As I read Calvin Robinson's memoir, I realized the historical interest of these ageing pages. The more I read, the more I became absorbed with the possibilities. In my quest for more information, several librarians provided invaluable help. James Cusick, Curator of Special Collections at the University of Florida, brought to my attention that a previous form of this manuscript was in the rare book room at his library. A cousin, Ralph Robinson, had provided that copy, which was incomplete. Historians had been using it as the only account of the Civil War in Florida written by a resident who sided with the Union. My copy revealed the whole story and offered information impossible to find anywhere else.

Calvin Robinson wrote this book; I merely modernized some of the grammar and divided the work into chapters with subheadings to orient the reader. In all else it is consistent with his original handwritten manuscript. He had things to say, burning in his heart, that future generations need to hear. He cared deeply about these United States.

— Anne Robinson Clancy

I

VERMONT ROOTS

May 20, 1865
Jacksonville, Fla.

*M*y Dear Friends:

Although some time has elapsed since you made the request, and I made the promise that I would write you an account of some of my experiences in Florida during the rise and progress of the late rebellion, I trust my compliance at this time may prove fully satisfactory, especially since I shall endeavor to make up for my delay by entering into more detail than I could have found time to do had I immediately complied with your request.

I was born in Vermont,[1] as perhaps you are already aware, and resided in that state till I was twenty-five years of age. My native town is Reading, in Windsor County; I received my education at the Springfield (Vt.) Wesleyan Seminary and the University of Vermont.

On account of ill health, however, I was obliged to discontinue my studies at the University during my junior year. But such was my standing while in that institution that in after years this old college, without any solicitation on my part, conferred on me the degree of Master of Arts.

Soon after leaving college, I engaged as teacher in the first-named institution, intending to make teaching the profession of my life. But the confinement of the school room soon so impaired my health that I was compelled to give up what was to me a most delightful occupation and engage in more active pursuits, and in February 1853 I went into business with Speare, Burke and Co. of Boston, wholesale oil merchants, and after two years became a partner in that concern.

On the 1st day of March 1855, I married Elizabeth Seymour of Burlington, Vermont. After some four years residence in Boston, I was again compelled to change my residence and business on account of ill health. The harsh climate of Eastern Massachusetts proving too severe for me, and being threatened with pulmonary difficulties, I resolved to change my residence to a latitude less rigorous; and in December 1857, I came to Florida. The following autumn I began the business of merchandising in Jacksonville.

Commencing under very favorable auspices and doing a larger business than had been carried on by any of the merchants then trading here, I necessarily met some opposition from my neighbor merchants; but, aside from this, I had no personal enemies in this country until the beginning of the excitement of secession.[2]

Tensions Tighten

After the John Brown raid and particularly after the breaking up of the Charleston Convention by the southern fire-eaters, the South began to be uncomfortable as a residence for northern men. The bitterness of the slave-holders became daily more manifest.

During the summer of 1860 and while the Presidential Campaign was going on, I was at the North visiting friends and buying goods. On my return to Jacksonville I found that some of the hotheads had been circulating the rumor, in my absence, that I was an "abolitionist." This term, in southern vocabulary, signified everything that was vile and abhorrent to southern people.

An abolitionist in the South was one who was supposed to be engaged in everything that was low and mean, and, particularly, inducing slaves to leave their masters or causing them to be insubordinate and incendiary. This charge against me was met and repelled by my friends, of whom I was so fortunate as to have a fair share. I never took the trouble to deny it myself.

After the election of Abraham Lincoln the more bitter and

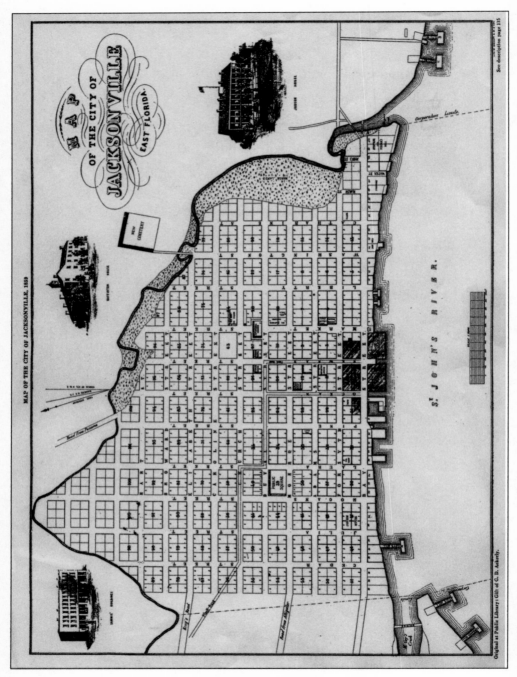

Map of Jacksonville, 1859

From T. Frederick Davis' *History of Jacksonville, Florida and Vicinity, 1513 to 1924*. The Florida Historical Society, 1925.

violent of the slave-holders and politicians began to use their utmost endeavors to arouse and "fire the southern heart." They succeeded admirably with the more inflammable portion of the people; but up to the time of the passage of the ordinance of secession [January 10, 1861], the more candid and sensible portion, composing at that time the majority of the community, were opposed to the movement.

Movement Toward Secession

A state convention was called by the Florida legislature of 1860 to meet at Tallahassee to take into consideration the duty of Florida under the circumstances. Most of the delegates to that convention were elected as Union Men. In our county (Duval) we elected two men to represent us who pledged themselves to go for Union to the last.

They had been at Tallahassee but a short time, however, before the rumor came to us that they were both going for disunion with their whole influence. When this news was confirmed, a number of the merchants of Jacksonville met; and, in consternation at the crisis to which we were being precipitated— question among ourselves what should be done to avert it.

It was finally decided to send three of our number to Tallahassee to expostulate with our delegates, and if possible to induce them to change their course before the final act of secession should be passed. I was one of the three thus appointed, but we found it as useless to talk to our delegates as it would have been to plead with lamp-posts in the streets.

On the 10th of January 1862 the ordinance of secession was passed by the convention. On the first ballot it was carried by only two majority, but afterwards all but seven persons signed the ordinance. Some noble spirits in that convention, prominent among whom were Col. Geo. T. Ward and W.G.M. Davis, fought secession to the very last, finally closing up the contest by making a strong effort to have the act referred to the people for their ratification. But this failed. The people would not have approved it, and the fire-eaters on the floor of the convention knew it. John P. Sanderson, our delegate in that convention, himself drew the ordinance.

After the passage of the act the number of adherents to the cause rapidly increased. The Union Men, however, for two or three months afterward continued to utter their sentiments of opposition to the movement; but gradually the reign of terror gained full sway, and the time came when for a northern man to utter openly his love for the Union would be almost suicide. Men who were born and reared in the South could speak against secession long after it was unsafe for northern men to do it.

II

EMERGING
CONFLICTS

Winter 1861

*I*t would be difficult to give an account of occurrences from this time forward to convey an adequate idea of the situation to one who has never witnessed the growth of civil war in the midst of a people.[3] Gradually, one after another, your neighbors would come out and join the current sentiment, moved by various influences of business advantage, personal influence, or popularity or notoriety. Some were impelled by the very force of the prevailing excitement until one hardly knew whom to trust.

Men with whom you talked today freely, and who were

firm in their opposition to the prevailing madness, would tomorrow boldly declare themselves in favor of secession, until the number of friends of the Old Flag became so small, and the stability of these so uncertain, that it was dangerous to talk "Union talk" with anybody.

If perchance you had made a special confidant of your sentiment to some neighbor whom you had considered more than commonly stable and firm, it was more than likely you would soon find your friend taking a front rank, perhaps because of his tardiness in coming out, becoming all the more zealous and active in his advocacy of secession. Your alarm and sense of insecurity became so much the greater because you had freely opened your heart to him, and now your fear was that he should "give you away!"

Indeed, in this manner were the Unionists all betrayed and their real sentiments fully known. Soon it came to the point that *silence was a crime.* It was believed naturally enough that "he who was not for secession was against it," and he who did not openly avow himself in favor of secession was counted an enemy of the South. For this reason many who were heartily in sympathy with the Union would utter sentiments of hostility to the Old Flag, especially in the presence of those who, they knew, were watching them and eager to catch something from their lips that could be used against them.

Indeed, all loyal men, at last—from being silent in the presence of those advocating rebellion—came to acquiesce more or less in what was said. They did this for their own personal safety or in behalf of the helpless bairns [children] which in these terrible times were so dependent upon them for their safety.

But, notwithstanding this silence and sometimes apparent acquiescence in the sentiments of bold advocates of southern views, I and all those few faithful men who were known to me during all these terrible days as staunch Unionists were distrusted and proscribed for what was believed to be our real sentiments. Emissaries were even sent to watch us and to interview us for the purpose of discovering some act or drawing from us some expression, word, or thought that could be construed at an unguarded moment to be hostile to the southern cause. Even eavesdropping was resorted to, and toward the last, we did not dare to talk without first examining to see that there was no possibility of our words being picked up through some keyhole, door crack, or around a corner.

Unionists' Secret Meetings

For this reason, a certain few noble spirits, for the sake of an opportunity to exchange views or to comfort each other or to discuss the news of the stirring events that were going on at the front of the contending armies, fell into the habit of going together every Saturday during the terrible winters of 1861 and 1862 into the neighboring hammocks with the ostensible purpose of hunting squirrels. After the early morning hunt was over, we would gather under some wide-spreading oak, and, sitting or lying on the thick carpet of autumn leaves, would talk "Union talk" freely "with no one to molest or make us afraid."

Notwithstanding our caution, there seemed to be no mis-understanding on the part of our zealous neighbors as to the sen-timents of every member of our little circle of loyal men, and each of us was often made to understand the suspicions that were entertained of our disloyalty to the Confederacy by various means—often open threats in the streets. On one occasion I met one of the more excitable of the "new government" adherents, who was somewhat under the influence of liquor at the time. He exclaimed, "Robinson, you d——d traitor! You ought to have your throat cut!"—showing plainly what he and his confreres thought when sober.

Public meetings at the Court House were called, and large gatherings of citizens more or less prominent in the community would volunteer their great eloquence to arouse the people who gathered. They spoke of the great importance of the revolution that was taking place—the righteousness of their cause, the Yankees' weakness and pusillanimity, and the great ease with which they should conquer the Northerners and secure southern independence. They charmed their hearers with their glorious portrayals of the delightful state of things they should have when the Confederacy was established and recognized by the civil pow-ers of the earth, exhorting all to great diligence against the trai-tors in their midst that were working up the negroes to sedition and slaughter.

These valiant men (most of them never showing their valor except in loud talk) vied with each other to see which could show the greatest patriotism in devising plans to bring out the people on the side of secession and to exhort everybody to "defend their homes and firesides" against the incursions of the enemy. But it was never made quite clear how or where or when the enemy would present themselves.

It was declared especially necessary that the citizens of Jacksonville should be enrolled into military companies and drilled to act as home guards. A captain was appointed at one of these meetings to muster and drill them. All citizens able to bear arms were called upon to appear at a certain hour, and some old Springfield muskets, altered over from flint locks, were procured, and the young, the middle-aged, and the gray-headed men of the town were formed in motley lines, with their guns standing in as many different directions as the stalks in a canebreak after a storm.

After this patriotic movement was set on foot, it was discovered that only a part of the men able to walk the streets were in these lines. At another public meeting it was declared that *every man* should come out and "show his hand." A somewhat noted character who was particularly demonstrative in his show of patriotism at these meetings was found to have figured quite prominently in the Kansas troubles of some years before. He declared that if the group would give him charge of this matter, he would "bring out the last man or know the reason why."

Under this high pressure of affairs, the Union Men, after some considerable talk among themselves, concluded that it would do no harm to assemble in the nearby grove and carry a gun for an hour a day as long as there was no organization or allegiance to any particular authority required (and there never was any). Since business was at a dead standstill and we needed the exercise, we cheerfully presented ourselves and bore the musket as valiantly as the most patriotic among them. Besides, it occurred to some of us that possibly at some future time we might have an opportunity to make a stand for the Old Flag we loved. Should this be the case, we knew that any skill we might acquire in the use of arms would be of no damage to us.

This practice was kept up but for a short time with any vigor or regularity. It became somewhat of an old story, and it was probably concluded that with the skill we had acquired with those terrible weapons, all that was necessary was for us to keep our muskets at our houses and ready if called upon in a dire emergency; and drilling pretty much ceased as newer excitements came up.

III

REBEL VIGILANTE

A little later on there was a movement made to organize a military company of younger men. A number of these individuals were northern men and Unionists, and some few were Germans who had no sympathy with secession. Believing the majority of this group to be loyal at heart, I joined the company. I had the advantage of considerable military training at a military school in Vermont, and so I drilled a squad of these fellows a few times. We procured a supply of old Harpers Ferry rifles with flint locks for our practice. They were a good army rifle with the exception of an obsolete flint lock. We elected for our captain a native of South Carolina and one of the noblest hearted young men I ever knew among the southern people. He was chosen on account of his very decided conservatism and his indifference towards the southern cause.

We were not mistaken in our opinion of him, for he took as little part in the war throughout the years as it was possible for him to do. We, however, refused all regular organization or enrollment. At one time an attempt was made to wheedle this company into enrollment as a "home guard." It did not go so far, however, as to require any individual opinions or protests. Our captain informed us quietly that it was a "trap to get us enrolled into the Confederate service," and he advised us to have nothing to do with it, which was fine with the whole company.

I believed that this company of young men, at least the large majority of them, if forced to take sides in the conflict, would have declared for the Union cause. At one time I felt so well assured of their allegiance that I took steps very quietly to procure the hammers and nipples necessary to alter our rifles and put them into a more serviceable condition should we ever have an opportunity to strike for the Old Flag. Now the fear was that the Confederacy, which was greatly in need of arms, would take our guns from us. I therefore very quietly took the new hammers out of our rifles and threw them into the St. Johns River, where the Confederates never found them.

Rebel Terror Tactics

Among the many early expediencies of the Rebels to test

the loyalty of all the citizens was a proposition that all the north-ern-born residents of the city should take the oath of allegiance to the Southern Confederacy. There was, however, enough loyal-ty left in the hearts of the northern men (and desire not to com-promise themselves by so decided a step) that the measure met a careful, but decided opposition, and the idea was soon quietly dropped.

But the excitement waxed on, and the feeling became more and more bitter with many of the southern people no doubt actuated by sincere motives and sentiments of what they believed to be pure patriotism; but there was always, all over the South a large element of ruffianism—the necessary outcome of the dominating spirit of slavery and the idleness of the young men. Many were profligate and drunken ruffians who had every-thing to gain and nothing to lose. Every community had many of these characters, and they formed the most prominent element of the vigilant committees. The outrages and cruelties commit-ted by these gangs upon the Unionists and their families remain untold, for the most part.[4]

Jacksonville had her Vigilant Committee, and their histo-ry of operation in the town before it fell into the hands of the Union forces was not much different from that of other places in the South. One line of action adopted by these gangs in Jacksonville was to terrify the northern merchants whom they suspected of not being sympathetic with the southern cause and to make levies upon them of large sums of money.

Their first attempt was upon a young hardware merchant from New York who had established a nice little business in Jacksonville shortly before the war broke out. The committee sent one of their number to "interview" this merchant. He was told that he was believed to "be unsound in his loyalty to the South" and that it was proposed to take charge of him and his effects. The young merchant protested that he was a noncombatant, that there had been no occasion for him to announce his sentiments, and that he merely tended to his business and was NOT an enemy of the South. Moreover, he would do anything they required to show his loyalty.

His visitor left him with the assurance that they would consult with "the authorities" and call upon him again later. Immediately, the young man called a prominent lawyer in the city and employed him to make the best terms that he could with these fellows. The result was that he was permitted to continue the management of his own affairs by paying them fifteen hundred dollars. He paid the money.

This endeavor succeeded so well that the gang tried it on me, expecting I presume, a large contribution to their coffers, as I had a much larger business. They sent one of their number to test my loyalty and to try my mettle. But I did not scare "worth a cent." I don't know any reason for my boldness except that my conscience most fully and emphatically approved of the course I had pursued. Every day I made it a matter of prayer that Providence would guide my course and give me wisdom every hour.

The man sent to me was a six-foot ruffian who had been a livery stable keeper in Jacksonville and who previously had made a narrow escape in the United States courts for robbing the mails. He met me in front of my store as I returned from dinner one day and announced that he had been sent to talk with me. He said that my conduct had been watched for some time back, and the committee had come to the conclusion that I was an Enemy to the South. They had decided to confiscate my property and to "take care of me."

I listened to his statements, and when he had got through, I looked him directly in the eye and told him that I had been harassed enough already till I was tired of life, that I did not care how quickly they came for me. I declared that I did not care to live, but one thing they should rest assured of: I would take some of his crowd with me. I was prepared for anything they might do, and they could come at any time, day or night, weekday or Sunday. He made no reply to this, and after a moment, I turned and left.

I was perfectly cool and unexcited when I said this, and I meant most emphatically what I said. We are told that "a rabbit will fight when cornered," and I was cornered. The bold course I had espoused would be suicidal in the long run unless some way of escape presented itself, because as the Confederacy became more strong and as supporters of the southern cause became more assured, they would annihilate any obstacle in the path. But the members of this self-constituted ruffian committee were cowards all and would quail in the presence of a really desperate and determined man.

As it resulted, however, it gave me time. It delayed levies or contributions or taxes for the present only. Perhaps at some future day, the "gang" would precipitate a more severe retribution upon me, but in a more cowardly manner.

IV

My Protection
Plans

One thing, which had no doubt to do with my safety and immunity from assault and outrage, was the fact that I had the reputation of being uncommonly expert with the pistol, as well as being very cool in emergencies.

During the evening and night after the above conversation, I began to realize, perhaps more than I had previously done, the extreme hazard and the almost hopelessness of my role. I felt, however, that I would not flinch for a moment from a single-handed encounter with these ruffians. I was armed every moment with the most efficient weapons with which I was most effective, so I did not dread any encounters with the gang in open daylight. But when I thought of my poor wife and two little boys (the oldest not yet four years of age) and how unprotected all of us were against any night attack these fellows might make on my home, for the moment, I became very sad and despondent.

I thought over my situation carefully. The Union forces had now captured Hilton Head and had extended their expeditions along the coast southward. I believed that they would soon enter the St. Johns River and take possession of our town. If I could make a bold and resolute stand to keep the mob at bay for a little while longer, I could escape the thraldom under which I was groaning. But I needed a plan to protect family against a night attack, their favorite way to dispose of difficult men.

It was not long a question in my mind. I had chosen to play a bold game. I decided to continue the policy I had begun and to fight it out, making it as expensive as possible to them should they attack me at any time. Immediately I proceeded to put my home it a more defensible condition.

I fixed a bell at the head of my bed, an arrangement so that no one could open either of my gates to my enclosure after nine o'clock at night without ringing that bell. Then I cut a trapdoor in the floor of a large closet located in the lower part of the house. I arranged it all so that I could open it in an instant and drop down and close it after me.

My house stood up nearly three feet from the ground and was underpinned with open-work of brick. So I could move

around readily there and see anyone within several yards of the
house through the interstices of the brickwork. Adjoining the
closet was the living room with a front window, which looked
out onto the entry walk. I then fastened the lower front window
up about six to eight inches and lowered the blinds to mask the
opening. I kept a heavy revolver under my pillow, and one of the
Sharps nine-inch breach-loading pistols lying by the new trapdoor, and the pistol was self-capping with cartridges.

My plan was, if wakened by the bell in the night, to step
quickly to a front window, where I could see plainly if any number of men were in front of or near the house. If anyone was present, I would seize the revolver and descend to the window below,
and, turning the slats of the blind slightly, get a view of some of
them, and discharge as many chambers of my revolver there as I
could do effectively, and be away quickly before they could bring
their revolvers or rifles to bear on the spot. Then I would descend
through the closet's trapdoor, grabbing my breach-loader as I
went. Through the wall's openings I could fire at the first man I
spotted, then move to another spot and fire again, continuing as
long as there were objects to shoot at.

I knew I could very quickly disperse any crowd of men
who would engage in such an expedition. I could load and fire
the breach-loader ten times a minute with great accuracy. I could
make them think that there was a squad of men under that
house! After making all these arrangements, my wife and I slept
without undressing each night. I had already made a ready way

of escape for her and the little ones, down a back way and out through a neighbor's lot.

State of Readiness

I had fully determined this procedure in case the mob came in one of their cowardly night attacks. I never went out of the house after nightfall, and we carefully lowered all curtains before lighting up any room. My bell arrangement no doubt had a wholesome effect; it sounded but once.

That one time I was awakened at night with its sharp ring. I sprang to the window with revolver in hand and, looking out, saw in the dim moonlight the city marshal and his assistant standing at the front gate. I had no fear of the regular authorities. I slipped downstairs and out a side door, and in a moment was in front of him with my revolver under his nose. He sprang back startled when I barked out, "*What* do you want?" The marshal mumbled that he had chased a runaway nigger up there and thought that he dodged into my lot. I said, "No man can come into my lot and I not know it: he ain't here." "No, no, he ain't here," says he. The sound of the bell and my sudden appearance surprised both men not a little.

I heard a few days afterwards that the marshal had reported downtown that "Robinson had some d——d infernal machinery about his house," and that it would not do to go fooling around there in the night. (Part of the bell fixture and the trapdoor arrangement are still in place now, and I keep the breach-loader yet.)

One worrisome area was that I had a large stock of goods on hand yet unsold. In the fall of 1860, after making my season's purchases, I had $70,000 worth of goods in the store and the warehouse. I then owned two large two-story brick stores standing on the ground now occupied by Astor's block and had twelve clerks to help me run the business. I also owned a two-hundred-foot-long large warehouse standing in the rear, a building which was thirty-six feet wide and extended back to my wharf.

The General Store of Calvin Robinson in Jacksonville, Florida, located on the corner of Bay and Hogan Streets.

V

CURRENCY
CONCERNS

I had not sold very largely from the warehouse goods when the war broke out. Then I grew more and more concerned about the currency which was in circulation. There were three different types of currency: Confederate money, state money issued for war purposes, and a great deal of railroad money, which I believed to be worthless, so I decided to shorten up my business by putting out of sight the largest portion of my best goods and to discharge clerks.

I soon closed the front doors of my store and sold only a few goods from the back doors and retained only two clerks, my best friends. One was Mr. Parker, who had come with me to

Florida and had served as my confidential clerk and friend all this while. The other was from St. Augustine, the son of a Polish exile. I had the fullest confidence in the loyalty of these two men, and with their assistance, I put out of sight nearly all of my stock, leaving only a small show on my shelves. The rest of my goods we packed in boxes and stored them in the warehouse, covered with empty boxes so it would appear that I had but few goods on hand.

My object in this was twofold: I found that ship stores, anything that could be used for encampment equipage, and clothing for soldiers, were going soon to be in very great demand to supply the Confederate troops. I knew if it were known that I had these items, I should be importuned to sell them to the Confederacy, and if I refused, they would take them, of course. As it was, two levies were made on me just before our city was taken by the Union forces. One, of ship stores to be used on board a river steamer which was in the Confederate service, and the other, of shovels, picks, and other material for camps and entrenching purposes. The fellow who enforced these levies claimed to be acting for the Confederate government.

They simply notified me that they were ordered to "press" these goods wherever they could be found. I sent a clerk to take a memorandum of them. I never got anything to show for these goods except this memorandum, and I have it now. This was just before the arrival of the Union forces and the occupation by them of the city of Jacksonville.

Another objective I had in packing away these goods was

to try to get them off to Savannah to sell for English exchange, which would be more useful than the currency then afloat in Florida. I went to Savannah and engaged rooms in the store of my commission merchant there, so he could store and show the goods.

Upon my return to Jacksonville, I made every effort in a quiet way, as no regular line was then running, to charter a steamer to take these goods up to Savannah. The captains would promise to take them in a few days, but then would fail to appear. At last I went to an old captain of a large tugboat who was very friendly to me and who was obligated to me for many material favors. I asked him to tell me frankly why he did not fulfill his promise; and he informed me that he could *not* take my goods, that he was prevented. He would not tell me by whom and for what reasons, but referred me to the collector of the port. I went to the collector and asked him what there was to prevent my shipping articles to Savannah. He replied that "we have concluded that you must sell your goods *here*." Says I, "Who are 'we' that presume to interfere in my affairs?" He said, "You will find out perhaps, but it would be best for you if you could keep pretty quiet and make no further effort to get your goods to Savannah. Your goods may be wanted *here*."

I knew very well who the "we" were. It was the same Vigilant Committee who sent the party to interview me. The steamboat men had been notified not to transport goods for me out of the state of Florida. So the lines were being drawn closer every day, and every day rendered my situation more precarious under the role I had undertaken to carry.

Rebel Persuasion Tactics

The Confederate authorities were building near Jacksonville a gunboat for their naval services. In the construction of this vessel they required considerable bar iron. They had exhausted the town's meager supply of this material, except for that which I had in my stores, and I had a large quantity.

They sent to me a prominent iron worker in town, with whom I had been quite friendly, to try and get this iron for the gunboat. I refused to sell the iron except for cash down since they were building the boat on the credit of the Confederacy while giving receipts only for materials and had little or no money.

The iron worker "reasoned" with me long and faithfully, but I was firm. I told him I had been interfered with in my business by certain parties already, and I had become a little desperate. I was determined to manage my own affairs; after all, the goods were *mine* and I should not part with them except on my own terms. He said, "Robinson, you are right."

The operations of this Vigilant Committee, and indeed its very existence, were not known to many of the citizens of the town up to the arrival of the Union forces in the St. Johns River. An organization of that character would not have been approved by a large number of our best citizens, especially those who had something of the old Union spirit left in them. There were more of these than I dared to hope for in that reign of terror which preceded the arrival of the Union gunboats. As the political sky had become darker, people had been more and more silent and careful about unburdening themselves to each other.

During 1860, the last year prior to the Civil War breaking out, I had, in connection with my merchandising, carried on the lumber business. I set up my lumber mill where the depot of the Jacksonville and Fernandina Railroad now stands. The spring and early summer of 1861 were the last months that I continued my trade, because the money currency, in my judgment, had become worthless.

I put away in my safe every dollar of southern bank money which I received.[5] Using the Confederate and state money issued for war purposes, along with the railroad money, I continued to buy logs and I kept my sawmill running a long time after all the other mills stopped. The lumber manufactured I piled in my mill yard nicely and covered it with sheds, believing that when the war was over, southern pine lumber would bring high prices and would be a much safer investment than the aforesaid currency.

My New Banking System

But the bank bills, as fast as they accumulated, were packed away safely in the following manner. I took wine bottles, and, wadding up the bills, put them into these bottles, tamped them down with a ramrod until the bottle was full. I then corked them, sealed the cork, and hid them away. Each bottle held from $800 to $1000.

After these accumulated to a number containing in all over twelve thousand dollars, I found them to be a sort of elephant on my hands and was at a loss to know how to dispose of them. If I should be made a prisoner by the Confederate authorities, there was no way to take my "treasure" along with me. Neither could I take the bottles if I should attempt to flee the town or the country.

There was great danger that, being apparently so obnoxious to the ruling spirits of the town and especially to the lower stratum of society, my store or house or both might be destroyed by fire. Indeed, I expected this: every morning I awakened with a deep sense of relief to find that these buildings were still standing. What should I do with my bottled treasure?

I finally decided that I would bury the bottles in my garden. And then whatever happened, even if obliged to flee the country, I perhaps could [come back after the war and] uncover my riches! For I thought it probable that the banks of the South might not ride out the storm, some of them. But to bury this money and *be absolutely certain that no one saw me do this* was a thing a little difficult to accomplish. There were parties living on two sides of me that I knew were zealous in the southern cause. I did not dare to bury it in the night for fear that I should be suspected certainly if seen digging there at that time.

Finally, I became quite engaged in hoeing up my garden and transplanting certain trees from one part to another. And one apple tree, about an inch and a half in diameter, which I had been trying to raise, I took up and set out in my backyard in a nice open space. For this purpose I dug a large hole and carried and dumped into it several large baskets full of rich earth and chip manure from various parts of the grounds.

One of these basketsful I procured on the east side of the washroom at the back part of my buildings, the tree being on the west side. On my way through the washroom, having the bottles in readiness there, I just put them into the center of the soft earth in the basket, covered them, and then carried and dumped the whole into the ample cavity in the ground, threw on some little soil, and set out the tree very nicely, filling in the earth around it to form a trough for water, which I poured in, so that the tree should be *sure to take root.*

Thus deposited, this money lay for many weeks in what under the circumstances I conceived to be the safest bank in the South until suddenly drawn out one night at midnight at a most exciting period in the history of our city.

VI

UNION GUNBOATS
APPEAR

*T*oward the latter part of the winter of 1861 and the spring of 1862, the expeditions sent out by the Federal forces at Hilton Head had proceeded southward along the coast as far as Cumberland Sound, and they were threatening Fernandina. When the news came to Jacksonville that the gunboats were off Fernandina, great excitement prevailed in our city.

A day or two later, word came that they had captured that valorous city, with the Confederate soldiers and the home guards all hurrying to the mainland on the appearance of the fearful gunboats in Cumberland Sound, without firing a gun. For many days, the greatest confusion prevailed in Jacksonville.

Straggling soldiers in considerable numbers came in from the Fernandina stampede, bringing with them the most exciting accounts of the rapidity and terror of those gunboats and of the narrow escapes they had made from captivity by them in the very marshes back of the town: One man said that the gunboats would "run anywhere where there was a heavy dew!"

Many families at once commenced leaving Jacksonville, hurrying their effects towards Lake City and other points along the railroad. News soon came that the Yankees were at the mouth of the river, that the terrible gunboats were already feeling their way towards our city. Our valiant soldiers who had been stationed at or near the mouth of the river "to defend our homes and firesides," and who for many weeks had been fortifying the coast and river to make it impregnable, came straggling upstream in boats and by land. These men swarmed into town, leaving the results of their long weeks of toil at the mercy of the Yankees, without firing a gun!

The Confederate gunboat was burned on its stocks as a "military necessity," to prevent its falling into the hands of the Federals. A large number of the ruffian portion of the population, which consisted mostly of members of the Vigilant Committee who had little or no property to be burned, insisted on leaving the town and that everybody should flee to the country.

Now the wildest excitement prevailed! Every sort of vehicle in town was pressed into service hurrying household goods and merchandise towards the depot. Families, hurrying to and fro, were packing off in the greatest haste!

This panic extended to nearly all the southern population, but most of the northern citizens and some of the larger property holders among the southern people objected to leaving the city and even drove off some of the most sanguine advocates of burning the city. But, in the midst of all this excitement, there were a *few citizens* who were *particularly unmoved*, even though threatened with vengeance if they stayed.

There was no terror in those gunboats or in the Old Flag for them! Their faces were calm and stoic while their very souls were ready to burst with joy at the thought of the deliverance at hand! O! did they not struggle to keep from shouting aloud for joy! But, though their countenances wore the expression of an apparent and studied indifference, it was impossible that the Rebels could not see the effort they were making to hide their delight. Many were the threats made against them.

Burning Fears

Some days elapsed before the gunboats, feeling their way along cautiously, reached the city. Some four days elapsed after they crossed the bar and entered the river.[6] During the interim, word came back from the Rebels in the country that my property and the large hotel property in the city were to be burned. I heard it several times, but could not at first learn who made the threat, or how and by whom the burning was to be done. [7]

Afterwards, parties returning from the country who were

friendly to me assured me that my property and that of the Judson Hotel were to be destroyed by the Rebel forces. My best and trusted Union friend and confidant, Judge Philip Fraser, who resided next door to me would be murdered by these troops along with me if we were found in town. It was said the Rebel forces were coming to burn the numerous sawmills and the large quantities of lumber to be found in our neighborhood.

VII

TERROR REIGNS

$\mathcal{W}$e did not really credit this rumor, but prayed that deliverance by the arrival of the gunboats might speedily come. But when their coming was delayed and the report confirmed, my friend, Judge Fraser, with his family became thoroughly alarmed. The judge insisted on his family leaving the city and hiding in the woods.

Coming up from my store in the afternoon of this day, I passed his house and heard considerable commotion within. I called in and found his family very much excited by their fears and insisting that the judge should flee from the city at once. It was soon settled that he should cross the river in the opposite directions from that taken by the Rebels in their flight and then take refuge in an old unoccupied house standing near the bank of the river in the woods a mile or more below town. I sent my boat and colored man from the store to row him and his family across to this place of refuge.

Having assisted my friends out of the way of immediate danger, I turned my attention to my own safety and that of my family. Entering my house, I found my little wife calm and smiling, but *very pale*. I asked her if she had heard the news that had so excited her neighbors, and she replied that she had. I asked her if she wanted to cross the river out of harm's way. She replied that if I thought it best, she would go. After supper, my wife and I went out upon the front piazza and sat down in the calm moonlight to talk over the situation. She first broke the silence by saying, "It is a beautiful peaceful night. It don't seem as though there was any one in the world that wanted to harm us. If you will stay tonight, I will!"

I said, "If you feel so calm about it, I will risk it one night more and rely on my house fortifications for safety, hoping that the gunboats will arrive here before morning." So we stayed in our own home that night. The morning found us at our house undisturbed, but the gunboats still had not arrived.

We decided, however, to send our trunks, which had been packed for a long time for just such an emergency, down to the lower end of the city. Our faithful Irish manservant, who was always at my house whenever there was any extraordinary excitement during this reign of terror, took the trunks. He carried them down in the night to his own cabin in the border of the marsh, with instructions that if his house was likely to be burned, he was to drag them out into the tall marsh grass behind his house. He also buried some large chests of bedding in my garden that they might be saved if my house should be burned.

That afternoon, while at my store, a neighbor who sympathized with secession but was very friendly to me, came rushing into the store and exclaimed, "Robinson, what did I tell you! Those Confederate troops sent to burn the mills are here at the depot. You've got to leave at once or you will not live to see another morning!" I told him it was impossible, that I had not heard the train come in. He said that they came without sounding the whistle or making any noise in order to surprise the town. He urged me to leave instantly.

I started immediately for my house. One the way, looking up the street to the depot, I saw the troops, a rough-looking crowd of about five hundred in number, forming in lines at the depot.

Running into the house, I took time only to get my wife and two little boys, with their young colored nurse, caught a tablecloth and threw into it and tied up what bread and cold cooked provisions were at hand, seized my traveling shawl, and hurried down to the store wharf and into a boat. I had just gotten out a few yards into the river, when the column of troops marched down Bay street, and another column down the back of the town, and in a few moments the city was under a close military guard. Behind these troops, armed with rifles, followed several of the most prominent characters of our late Vigilant Committee. As they passed, one of them saw me and called my name with an oath and a curse.

We hurried across the river and down to my friend Fraser's place of refuge in the cabin by the river bank. As I came by the store, my faithful friend and clerk, Mr. Parker, came out and said he would not leave, but would stay by the store. He said, "I am an old man; they will not disturb me." So he and the young clerk, Ivanowski, locked themselves into the store.

For some weeks previous to this, I had employed two reliable men to watch my store and wharf during the nights, each armed with a double-barreled gun, under a pledge that they would shoot down anyone they should catch setting fire to the property. These men also were on duty that fearful night.

With my little family I took up quarters in the old house with friend Fraser, who gave us a hearty welcome to their humble abiding place. We reached there just as night came on. An hour or two after our arrival, while we were sitting on the floor eating some of the cold luncheon we had brought with us, we were startled by the sudden illumination of the surrounding woods. We looked out and discovered that the Confederates had begun their work of burning the steam sawmills in the neighborhood of Jacksonville. One which stood on that side of the river near where we had taken refuge seemed to have been the first set on fire. There were eight or ten of these mills, with millions of feet of sawn lumber within sight of where we stood. Soon all these were in flames, and their lights reflected back from the sky, then overcast with heavy clouds, was a fearful sight to look upon. The whole heavens seemed like billows of flames.

While gazing at this grand conflagration, some friendly colored people from a neighboring plantation, who knew of our place of refuge, came cautiously to us and informed us that there were several armed men creeping around in the bushes back in the woods. Fearing these fellows were some of our zealous friends of the Vigilance Committee who were hunting our place of refuge, we left our little ones sleeping on blankets on the cabin floor and crept out into the woods some rods along up the bank of the river and stood there, silently concealed in the bushes in a drizzling rain nearly all night, watching the progress of the conflagration.

My large white warehouse and the store in front were conspicuous objects on the river and were in plain sight from where we stood. Along towards midnight, we noticed a light approach the outer end of the warehouse on the wharf and stop where I had a large quantity of loose shingles piled up against the building. Presently we discovered a bright flame shoot up from the shingles, up the side of the warehouse, and then along the whole length of the roof. In ten minutes, the flames driven by the strong southerly wind had enveloped the whole building.

VIII

JUDSON HOUSE BURNS

These emissaries were some half dozen of the so-called southern chivalry, such as were found in every community in the south in those days—scions of broken-down southern aristocracy who had squandered their patrimony and, while they still laid claim to gentility, underneath a thin surface of the gentleman were simply brutal barbarians.

These fellows followed the battalion of Confederate troops into the city that night, went to the Judson House, as usual, where previous bills for entertainment were still standing against them unpaid, met the hostess, Mrs. O.L. Keene, politely set her fears all at rest by assuring her that there was no truth in the reports that the hotel was to be burned. They ordered supper prepared by her hands and ate it. But in less than an hour after they had finished their repast, they began their work of destruction by applying the torch to some old buildings adjoining, with a view to burning the hotel.

Mr. and Mrs. Keene, seeing that all was about to be destroyed, rushed to their private rooms and began bringing out some of their choice articles. Among them was a fine old mirror, which Mrs. Keene highly prized as a valuable heirloom in her family. Seeing one of the aforesaid young men standing in the rear, whom she had fed that night and often previously without money, she handed him the mirror. He assured her that her property would not be destroyed, and she begged him to carry it to a place of safety. He took the glass from her hands and turning from her deliberately smashed it to fragments on his knee. Then he ordered her not to remove anything more from the house. A few minutes later, the large Judson House, a grand wooden hotel that stood on the site of the present Everett House and belonged to northern men, was wrapped in flames.

Mr. Keene did, however, succeed in saving many articles of household goods from the hotel, carrying them to a knoll some three hundred yards west of the hotel beyond reach of the flames. He and his good wife stood guard over them till the daylight came and indeed till the gunboats arrived, making it safe to bring them back into town again. But as that band of ruffians who had perpetrated the pillage and burning in the city departed on the train at daybreak, they left one more evidence of their style of chivalry: They fired a volley at these inoffensive people—Mr. Keene and his wife—from the train cars as they moved out from the depot. One of their bullets passed through the brim of the hat which Mrs. Keene was wearing.

IX

OUR HOPELESS
SITUATION

*N*ow we knew that the rumors brought to us were true, and they would murder us if they could find us! We began to realize the hopelessness of our situation! Driven from our home, property and home destroyed, our hiding place probably known, no way of escape! So long a time having elapsed and no gunboats coming to our relief, they must have turned back! They were not coming! If we contemplated flight towards them, the retreating Confederates from the defenses down the river, which still filled it with boats, would make that retreat impossible! To flee by land thither, the Pottsburg and the Pablo with their impassable marshes would render our escape hopeless, worn and exhausted as we were. It was a dark hour!

While the store and warehouse were burning, we heard a dozen or more rifle shots and saw the flash on the outer end of the burning wharf. Were they firing at my poor friend Parker and his companion? We feared so, and so it proved. Later I learned that before setting the warehouse on fire, the mob captured my two watchmen and held them prisoners. Then they commenced their work of destruction. When they had fired the warehouse, they proceeded to the store. Taking a heavy timber, they battered down the front doors, and entering, lighted the gas burners, and then the rabble immediately commenced pillaging the goods. They continued for an hour, and then, piling up some cotton goods in the middle of the floor, they set fire to them, destroying the balance, store and all.

When the front doors fell in from the blows of the mob, Mr. Parker and the young man opened the safe and seized arm-loads of account books, and then fled from the back door, just as the mob entered the front doors. My two men hurried to my boathouse back of the burning warehouse, and they sprang into a boat and shoved it out into the river. The boat oars had been carried away. The Rebels believed I was in the store, and they had taken them to prevent my escape.

The young man [Ivanowski] was an excellent boatman and as brave as ever lived. Finding that they were being pursued, he seized a shingle and paddled on as fast as he could. As they passed out into the stream, the mob, finding the men had escaped, hurried around the burning warehouse out to the end of the wharf. Leveling their rifles upon the young man, they ordered him to halt. He says, "I won't do it," and pulled on. The mob commenced firing upon the boat.

Mr. Parker lay down in the bottom of the boat to escape the shots, and the young man bravely kept on. They fired some twenty shots after the boat without effect. But when Mr. Parker lay down, they thought it was me, and they exclaimed that they had killed the d——d Yankee. This I learned from the imprisoned watchmen who were there with them. The refugees hastened across the river and drew the boat up into the marsh grass as far as possible.

Leaving the account books, they sprang out and hurried to the woods as fast as possible to escape a boat that followed them closely across the river. They got separated in their flight, and the young man found his way to a plantation house some two miles away, which is now the property of Mrs. Alexander Mitchell. But Mr. Parker followed the main road toward St. Augustine and ran until he was exhausted and fell by the roadside.

Recovering a little and finding his pursuers were not in sight, he kept on toward the ancient city as fast as he could travel. He walked and wandered about all that night, all the next day, and the next night until midnight, when he reached the city and the home of Ivanowski, the brave young Pole clerk, who rowed him across the river. Here he received a hearty welcome from the good mother of the young man, but was immediately taken up with a brain fever, which continued nearly two weeks, most of which time he was delirious.

When the day dawned on our little band of refugees on the bank of the river, it found us in our hiding place, as hopeless a little company as the world ever sees. As the daylight came, the ladies (my wife, Mrs. Fraser, and her three nearly grown daughters) went back to the house, while the judge and I betook ourselves to the outer end of a long boat wharf that extended out into the river not far from the old cottage.

The land was cleared up, back from the wharf some distance, and standing at the outer end of the wharf, we were beyond the range of anyone who should attempt to fire upon us from the woods. Should anyone come into the opening to approach us, we had resolved to take a boat that lay by the wharf and make the best of our way towards the mouth of the river to the gunboats.

But escape by this way, as before stated, seemed impossible. And, as the morning advanced, we sat there silently contemplating the hopelessness of our situation. Our property and homes lay in smoldering ruins before us, and our enemies surrounded us on all sides, hunting us as though we were wild beasts—our helpless wives and little ones with us, without even a day's provisions. What could be added to render our situation more desperate? The gunboats, being so long delayed, we were forced to conclude, were not coming at all.

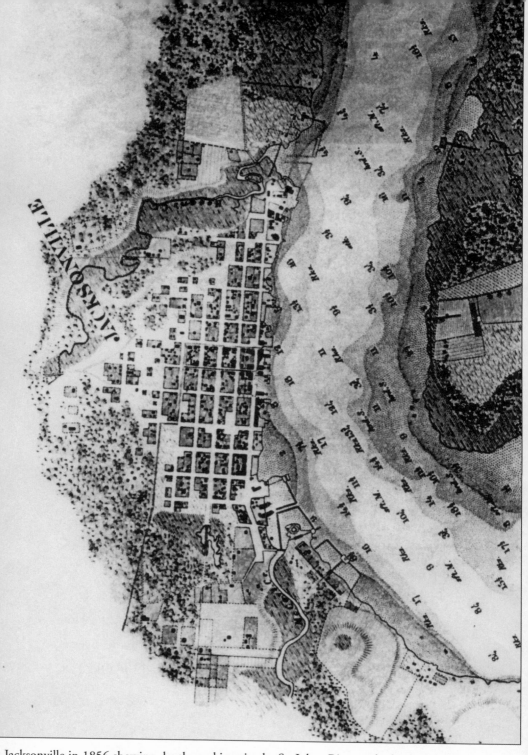

Jacksonville in 1856 showing depth markings in the St. Johns River and a layout of the town
From collections at the Jacksonville Historical Society Archives

X

DELIVERANCE

Thus we sat, plunged to as low a point of despair as mortals ever reach, when suddenly I noticed a commotion at the cottage! One of the women came out and ran around the farther end of the house. Another came out and was running towards us. I feared some of the guerrillas hunting us had entered the house in the rear. I called to her, "What is the matter?" She turned and pointed down the river.

And there, below the grassy point, loomed up a pair of schooner masts, moving slowly towards us. And just below, another and another: four of them! And over the foremost vessel, brightly floating against the morning sky, waved the Old Flag, which we had not seen for nearly two years! Never did greater joy more suddenly take possession of hearts in deeper despondency!!

Never again do I expect to feel such rapture till, perchance, if so permitted, I pass through the "Pearly Gates" into the New Jerusalem!!

I called the attention of my friend [Judge Fraser] to the sight, and never shall I forget the look on his face as he gazed a moment at the Old Flag. His countenance, pale and haggard to the extreme from weeks of anxiety and watching, in a moment lit up with such an expression of gladness as the conviction took possession of his soul that *help* had really come!

He sprang into the air and shouted, *"Thank God!!"* We both ran towards the cottage. An old citizen living near had wandered out from his house and made his appearance at the top of the knoll back of us just as the boats were discovered. In extreme cautiousness he cried out to the women who were coming out of our hiding place, "Go into the house. Tell the women to go into the house. They will think you are Rebel soldiers and will throw shells at you!"

Judge Fraser swung his hat and shouted, "Let them fire! It would be glorious to be killed with shells from under that Flag! We ran down to the house and called for *something white*. The ladies instantly brought out an old sheet that had wrapped our provisions, and seizing it we put it upon an old boat strut, and waved it aloft. In a moment it was answered by a white flag from the bow of the flagship!! When we waved ours, it would wave in answer! We had no further fear of *shots* from that quarter!

As they moved on up opposite us in the river, I sprang into a small boat. A colored man from a neighboring plantation came running down at that moment and offered to row me over to the vessels. (The colored men were always *nearby* when the Unionists were in trouble! *God bless them!)*

As we approached the rear gunboat, the *Isaac Smith*, I became timid, How was I to get on board that formidable vessel? But I ventured a "Hello" and was answered instantly from the forward deck, "Hello, what do you want?"

"I want to come aboard," I said. "What do you want to come aboard for?" he said. I replied, "I want to come aboard for protection and to give you all the information I can!" "Come aboard, come aboard," he answers, and immediately I heard the engine bell sound a stop, and the vessel slowed down. As I came alongside, several sailors lifted me on deck, and I ran to the upper deck and was met by Captain Nickerson, in command, and seizing his hand, I shouted, "God bless you! God bless you!" in the wildest state of excitement.

The noble captain, from my wild and haggard looks, was fearful that I had "gone daft," or would do so *soon*. He congratulated me on my escape and sought to quiet me a little. He asked me down into his cabin and had the steward set me out some wine, crackers, and cake. He asked me what was going on here, and what all that smoke meant. He begged me to remain there, to calm down, and told me that when they reached town, he would come for me. But that one cabin was not large enough for me! I was on deck a moment behind him and watched the town as we approached it.

As the vessels all circled into the harbor, Captain Stevens of the flagship *Ottawa* signaled the officers of all the boats and the military officers on board to come on board his vessel. When all had assembled, he invited me in, and after his introduction, he asked me to give an account of the situation in Jacksonville.

I did so and urged upon them the fact that there were many citizens in Jacksonville who were loyal to the Old Flag, or would be, should the threatening power of the Confederacy be lifted from them. After a short consultation among the officers, the captain announced that they had no orders to occupy our city. But under the circumstances, it was the unanimous judgment of the officers that they ought to land and take possession of the town.[8]

XI

First Union Occupation

March 1862

*T*he signal was given, and amid the cheering strains of "Yankee Doodle" from the bands, the troops on board the gunboats debarked—consisting of the 4th New Hampshire Regiment and a large number of Marines—who landed and took possession of the town, Colonel Whipple commanding.

The same evening the Yankee soldiers and sailors went over in boats and brought our families back to town. Our happiness was not a little increased to find that our homes were not destroyed, but saved through the strenuous efforts of a neighboring widow lady who was in good favor with the leader of the rabble. When they came to apply the torch to our houses, she pleaded that if they burned the houses of Judge Fraser or mine, it would certainly burn *her house,* which stood near. After much entreaty, she prevailed on them to postpone the job till some other night when the wind should be more favorable. So our homes were spared to us.

The presence of the Federal troops in Jacksonville brought to light a condition of sentiment that I had believed to exist all along. A number of residents who had been silent or who had even been in the state military service to help garrison the river and coast fortifications came out promptly on the arrival of the Union forces and declared themselves for the Union. Under the terrorism that had prevailed and grown more and more violent every day, many who were *really in sympathy with the government* had appeared to acquiesce in secession. Some had even been demonstrative in their support of Confederate usurpation.

Many well-known Unionists who had not been so pronounced in their sentiment did not leave the town on the approach of the troops that night, but hid themselves away as best they could till morning, when the mob who had made the night hideous with their lawless burning and pillage betook themselves to the country, loaded with plunder they had taken from my store. Some few belated ones, however, did not get off till the Union gunboats hove into sight—which sudden presentment accelerated the speed of their departure very decidedly.

I am informed by an aide de camp of General Trapier, who

A Jacksonville store catering to Union soldiers during an occupation
From collections at the Jacksonville Historical Society Archives

commanded the Confederate forces in Florida (whose letter I have now before me), that the burning of the sawmills and foundry only were ordered by Confederate authority; that the destruction of the Judson House and my property was strongly urged upon the general but that he refused to give the order. Yet their destruction was fully determined upon by a few individuals, not in any way connected with the army, but who believed they represented the wishes of many of the leading Rebels of Jacksonville when the troops left that day to carry out the said order.

On March 20, 1862, all loyal Unionists were called to register their names, and within two hours there were eighty-two names listed. A meeting was held of these persons, and C.L. Robinson was elected chairman. Appropriate resolutions were drafted for discussion on March 24, a meeting attended by locals and delegates from throughout Northeast Florida.[9] A large number of printed copies of the proceedings of the March 24 meeting and of this proclamation were sent to Fernandina and St. Augustine and elsewhere outside the lines of the Union forces wherever they could be conveyed for distribution.

One old patriot at St. Augustine lost his life in his zeal to get these documents to the interior of Volusia County. His name was Whitney. He was a blacksmith and a local preacher. He had been accustomed to make excursions out into the country, particularly in the southern portion of St. Johns and through Volusia County, visiting the people and preaching occasionally, and believed he had many friends throughout that district.

On his last visits through this neighborhood, he found his friends almost unanimously loyal to the Union. Some weeks had elapsed since that visit, but being anxious his friends should hear what had transpired, he took a quantity of the Proceedings and the proclamations and rode off over his accustomed route to carry to the people the glad news of a restoration to the peace and protection of the United States authority.

But this time his friends in the country did not "talk Union talk" as much as they did formerly. Indeed, the progress made by secession, the falling into line of the state of Virginia and other border states that had stood out for some time against the craze that was sweeping the South, and other influences that had been brought to bear upon them, had drawn these denizens of the far-off piney woods into sympathy with the wild movement. When the good old man came around, his mission was not well received.

They did not, however, confront him with their changed opinions but received him with apparent kindness and allowed him to proceed some distance down among the settlements, when a number of men gathered together, pursued and overtook the old man in the forests. They put a rope around his neck as he sat on his old horse, tied the other end high up to an overhanging limb, whipped up the animal and left him hanging in midair till he was dead.

I will also add a sequel to this incident. Just two years afterwards, one Murray, the ringleader of this gang, was taken

Soldiers and friends in an informal pose at a Union encampment in Jacksonville by the St. Johns River. From collections at the Jacksonville Historical Society Archives

prisoner by the Union troops, and the above facts coming to the knowledge of the commandant of the post at Jacksonville, he was tried by court-martial, sentenced and hanged, and his body buried where he was hanged, at the northeast corner of the tract now known as Riverside, a suburb of the city of Jacksonville.

On the 24th day of March, pursuant to notice given, the Unionists of the cities of Jacksonville, St. Augustine, and Fernandina, and many from the country near the cities and points up the river, assembled at the Court House and held their second Union meeting.[10]

The following is a true copy of their proceedings, which were printed and distributed at the time, several of which I now have in my possession.

PUBLIC MEETING

Agreeable to adjournment, the citizens of Jacksonville and vicinity met at the Court House on Monday, 24th March, at 10 o'clock, A.M., C.L. Robinson in the Chair, O.L. Keene, Secretary.

On motion, the following gentlemen were appointed by the Chair to prepare business for the meeting, to wit; John W. Price, P. Fraser, J.T. Mitchell, C.S. Emery, and J. Remington.

Said Committee reported the following which was accepted and adopted unanimously:

Whereas, For the security and happiness of the people of the State of Florida, it is necessary that a State Government be formed in accordance with the provisions of the Constitution of the United States, and of the State of Florida as it existed previous to the passage of the Ordinance of Secession, therefore:

Resolved, That in order to facilitate the formation of such a Government, a convention of the people be called, to meet at the city of Jacksonville, on the 11th day of April, A.D. 1862, to establish a State Government, elect a Governor and other State Officers, a Representative to Congress, or in their sovereign capacity to provide therefore as they shall deem best for their interest.

Be it further Resolved, That all the Counties and precincts of the State which shall think proper, be requested to send Delegates to said Convention.

Be it further Resolved, That under the benign influence of the Government of the United States, as it now exists over us, our property and lives are secure from the incendiary and assassin, and enjoy the protection and peace which are now ours.

Resolved, That a copy of these Resolutions be distributed throughout the State as extensively as possible.

All of which has been respectfully submitted.

John W. Price, Chairman

On motion of P. Fraser, the following was received and adopted unanimously; That the Citizens of the several Counties and Precincts will, on Monday, April 7, 1862, elect Delegates to attend the Convention to be holden at Jacksonville, April 10th, 1862.

On motion of P. Fraser, Esq., the Meeting adjourned *sine die.*

C.L. Robinson, Chairman

O.L. Keene, Secretary

Jacksonville, Fla., March 26, 1862.

On issuing this proclamation as above stated, General T.W. Sherman returned to Hilton Head and sent to our city a large reinforcement of troops to garrison the town.

These demonstrations of a purpose to protect the Union men in their movements, on the part of the military authorities, inspired all with the full confidence in the Union occupation, and we were proceeding without apprehension to carry out the suggestions of General T.W. Sherman and the resolution of the meeting of March 24 to reorganize the civil authority, by a convention of delegates to be holden on the 10th day of April, 1862.

The Union sentiment was gaining ground rapidly, and we were daily receiving congratulations and assurances from planters and others from Mandarin and Clay counties and various other directions through parties coming through the lines. Nearly all the whole country was in sympathy with us, and would support us and would exhibit their support just as far as their safety from the Rebel troops—who to the number of about one thousand, two hundred, were lying about ten miles west of Jacksonville—would permit.

XII

EVACUATION

*R*ebel Response

While these things were going on within the Union lines, the Rebels outside were doing all within their power to retain their hold upon the people. Colonel Floyd, at that time in command of Rebel forces in East Florida, issued a most bitter and threatening proclamation in reply to that sent out by General Sherman. Rumors were constantly coming in from outside, of the vengeance that awaited those of us who had been prominent in the Union conventions—particularly mentioning Judge Fraser and myself—that they would be better pleased to capture us than two of the highest officers at the post. A warning was brought to

Recrossing the St. Johns River with prisoners, wagons, and other captured stores (Mary E. Dickison, Dickison and His Men, 1890)

us by a person living about eight miles out that an expedition was planning to dash into town and capture us and make examples of us to intimidate others who were weak in their loyalty to secession.

But all this had no effect upon those of us who were, as we supposed, safely within the protection of the Federal forces, except that Judge Fraser and I were careful not to sleep in our homes in the suburbs of the city, but spent our nights in warehouses or somewhere near the river within the protection of the friendly gunboats.

Union Troops Evacuate

Such was the situation and the encouraging prospect held

out before us, when on the evening of the 7th of April (just three days before the day appointed for our convention of Union delegates), a preemptory order came from Hilton Head that *the town be evacuated and the troops return to Hilton Head immediately.*

The first intimation I had of this order came through an officer of General Wright's staff who came to my house at nine o'clock in the evening of the 7th and said that the town would be evacuated the next day at ten o'clock.

This intelligence fell on our ears like a *death knell!* It *was* a death knell to our reviving hopes! For months we had been in terror—threatened and persecuted—worn out with anxiety and watching, driven at last into the woods, and our property pillaged and burned, then anon rescued from our peril. Our hope had been revived and our hearts comforted with the reflection that we had been vindicated, and that our humble homes and a few comforts were still spared to us and our little ones were at last in safety. Now, suddenly like a thunderbolt from a clear sky, this order comes dashing to earth the last hope and banishing us from our homes and the few comforts saved from the wreck and sending us out, refugees and wanderers, to what we knew not where. This was indeed *hard!*

The officers made no suggestions and offered us no way of escape. The announcement stunned us! After his departure we sat paralyzed for an hour. At ten o'clock we were aroused by Colonel Guss of the 97th Pennsylvania Regiment with whom we had formed a pleasant acquaintance. He had anticipated our sad situation and came to tell us that a settler's schooner, just unloaded, was about to sail for New York. He also offered his regiment wagons to take to the boat anything we wished to save.

He brought with him several of his officers, and cheering us up to action, helped us to pack off some of the best and easiest-moved of our household stuff. We hurried, lest word had gone outside that the town was being evacuated and the Rebels taking advantage of the confusion, should dash in upon us, at least those of us on the outer border of the city.

Our Escape from Jacksonville

At midnight, having packed up and sent away to the schooner about one-third of our furniture, we left our home and betook ourselves again for safety to the warehouses near the gunboats.

My last act before leaving was to dig up the bottles of bank currency, which I had buried under the apple tree some ten weeks previously. I brought them in, and being in great haste, smashed the bottles into fragments in an old wood box. I fished out the wads of bills from among the broken glass, threw them into a pile, and wrapped them up in an old window curtain, tied the bundle up with a string, making it no larger than a man's head. I threw this bundle into a box of books that was just being nailed up. No one but my wife knew what the bundle contained. It traveled in that box of books to New York, and thence to my father's house in Vermont before it was taken out.

I will here add that while at this time I had but little faith in the value of this bundle. But afterward, during the war, I sold this money to brokers in New York for fifty-five to sixty-five cents on the dollar, thus realizing over seven thousand dollars from my deposit under the apple tree. These money brokers were buying up the cotton of the planters as the army advanced. The cotton planters preferred these bills to the greenbacks.

XIII

TRAVEL TRAVAIL

$\mathcal{T}$he next morning, Judge Fraser and I, with our families, were offered the hospitalities of the gunboat *Seneca* by its commander, Captain Ammen, as our escape vehicle to Hilton Head. As we left the city about nine A.M., a great commotion prevailed. Some twenty families were hurrying with their baggage to board the huge transport steamer the *Cosmopolitan*, which had been offered to convey such others as desired to leave Jacksonville.

We arrived at Hilton Head the next morning at ten A.M. Soon after our arrival, Lieutenant Sproston of the *Seneca* accompanied me on shore to see what could be found in the way of

73

quarters for our women and children. The few extemporized buildings which had been put up to accommodate the army commissary and quartermaster and hospital departments were all pretty well occupied. Everything else was in tents.

After a good deal of traveling from one place to another and being transferred from one officer to another, we were assigned our room about sixteen feet square, in the hospital building. We were given as many shuck mattresses as we wished to spread on the floor at night, on which to sleep. These were piled up during the day at the side of the room, three or four deep, and served us as seats. There was no other furniture. Two families consisting of thirteen persons laid down on these mattresses on that floor and slept at night, with no pillows or covering except such wraps as we carried with us. The weather was mild, however, and we got along with but little suffering for the ten days we remained at Hilton Head. The commissary furnished us our meals at a restaurant some three hundred yards from our quarters.

This was the best that could be done for us in that army camp, and was indeed much better than we expected possible. We were very grateful for the attention we received. All the officers and men in the camp treated our little band of refugees with the greatest respect and kindness, after so summarily being driven from our homes of comparative comfort.

Everywhere, we heard emphatic denunciations of the cruel and unnecessary order which had caused our stampede from those old homes of ours.

When the *Cosmopolitan* came in some days later with her large crowd of refugees aboard, they did not land, since it was easier to quarter these people aboard. There they remained on board till means were provided to send them northward.

At the time of our arrival at Hilton Head, the bombardment of Fort Pulaski was in progress and continued for nearly a week after that, when it surrendered. During this time General Hunter, commander of the Department of the South, was away at the scene of action, and nothing could be done toward securing passage to New York.

For several days after his return, we besought him to provide some means of transportation, but he could not determine anything. On the tenth day of our sojourn, Admiral Du Pont sent us word that one of his transports, *The Star of the South*, had just discharged her cargo and was to return immediately to New York.[11] When he offered us passage on her, we gratefully accepted his kind offer, and we were soon aboard. The noble admiral supplied the vessel with provisions and every needed comfort for the refugees numbering over a hundred, and, as I learned afterwards, at his own private expense. God bless the noble admiral!

Reception in New York, Summer 1862

We had a successful voyage to New York. The provost marshal general of the Department, Colonel J.F. Hall of New York, going thither on business, accompanied us on the voyage. We arrived at the steamer's dock in New York at four o'clock in the morning. The gallant provost left the vessel immediately on her arrival and went uptown. At seven o'clock, just as we were finishing breakfast, the colonel returned aboard, bringing his father, General Hall of New York, and several other gentlemen to see us. After a little conversation and learning of the destitution of most of us, they requested us to stay aboard until we should hear from them again.

At eleven o'clock in the forenoon, the general returned and informed us that he had been authorized to distribute us, some two or three families, among the leading hotels of the city. Here we would have the privilege of stopping without charge for ten days or two weeks till we could rest and hear from our friends and decide where to go. He also informed us that our case had been presented to the Chamber of Commerce at its session that morning, and a committee had been appointed by that body to solicit funds for our relief, and that they would call on us at our hotels the next day.

Hospitable Welcome

We went to the hotels to which we were assigned and were kindly received, given the pleasantest of quarters, and bade to make ourselves comfortable and at home.

The next day the committee called on us and left with each head of a family a check for from $150 to $250, according to the size of the family. They told us that the kind-hearted merchants of the city had contributed these funds that we could procure such articles as we might stand in immediate need of and to pay our way to our friends.

What noble conduct was this! Did it not feel like the sweet doors of Heaven on the hearts of these poor, broken-hearted and homeless people! Heaven knows it was appreciated, and this timely grand exhibition of the noble spirit of these noble men should not be lost to the history of that memorable period.

The city papers on the morning after our arrival were full of notices of our arrival and the incidents of our recent history with the fiery trials through which we had passed. Only one of these have I been able to preserve. It was an account of us after an interview with Judge Fraser.[12]

After remaining in the city of New York for a few days, the refugees scattered in different directions, most of them to their friends in the North. Having stopped here with my family for a week and becoming some-what rested from the fatigues and excitements of the few preceding weeks, I sent my family to father's house in Vermont.[13]

XIV

UNIONISTS UNITE

I went myself for a few days to Washington, where I met a number of the leading men of our party of refugees to consult together and take such steps as should seem best for our relief in the peculiar circumstances of our case. At Washington we also met several other gentlemen from other parts of Florida.

We soon found that the evacuation of Jacksonville was looked upon by the authorities there as a *great blunder* and greatly regretted by none more than by the noble President Abraham Lincoln! On calling upon President Lincoln, he assured us that he looked upon this moment in the light and said it was done without orders from the War Department and that it was a great mistake and he was sorry it had occurred. In his opinion, the town should have been held and made a base of operations for the control of the peninsula of our State to cut it off from the rebellious districts. He said that it should be retaken again as soon as troops could be spared from other operations for that duty.

Just at that time a heavy troop movement was being made in Virginia and in Tennessee, and the discouraging successes of General McClellan made it uncertain whether or not more troops would be needed at these more important points. So the day of our return to Jacksonville was deferred.

Towards autumn in 1862, the Eli Thayer enterprise of "armed occupation" was proposed: the enlistment of men to enter Florida and settle, a sort of confiscation of lands and distribution of them to those who would take and defend them. This scheme was approved by the Cabinet, and the matter turned over to the Secretary of War to work up. And there it hung. I apprehend that on entering into the details of the plan, the impracticability of the proposition became more apparent, and it went no further.

Our friend Fraser was appointed judge of the northern district of Florida at our request at that time.

In June the Direct Tax Act was passed, and L.D. Stickney from southwestern Florida, Colonel J.L. Sammis of Jacksonville, and Harrison Reed of Wisconsin were appointed commissioners under it to levy and collect this tax for Florida. A place on this commission was offered to me, but desiring to be free when the

Federal forces should again advance into East Florida (which it was expected would soon be done), I declined the office.

I needed to gather up the fragments of my wrecked business. But later in the season, sensing then that no immediate prospect of any further movement during the remainder of the year and feeling it necessary, on account of my health, that I should reside south during the winter months, I accepted the position of Assistant Assessor to the Tax Commissioners and went south on the sixth of December, 1862, after having spent most of the season with my family in my native state.

Prior to this, I was detained in New York some two weeks waiting for a transport to Hilton Head. No vessels but those in the government military service passed between these ports, and these passed back and forth as the exigencies of the service required. There were no regular lines at that time.

Cooper Institute Meeting

While waiting for a steamer in New York, I had the honor and the pleasure of participating in a grand Union mass meeting held in the Cooper Institute at the suggestion of citizens from the southern states who were tarrying in the city, mostly as refugees.

Notices appeared in all the leading papers of the city as follows, to wit:

> *Union War Meeting* under the auspices of citizens from Slave-Holding States: The Union-loving citizens of the city of New York, irrespec-

tive of party, are invited to meet with the under-
signed citizens of the States now in insurrection
against the Federal Government, at the *Cooper
Institute,* on Saturday evening, October 25th,
1862, for the purpose of giving an *Emphatic
Endorsement* to the efforts now being made by
the constituted authorities of the land to crush
this cruel and proscriptive rebellion:

These certainly will address the meeting:

Col. Andrew Jackson Hamilton of Texas

Hon. Philip Fraser of Florida

Hon. L.D. Stickney of Florida

Calvin L. Robinson of Florida

These men are expected to be present to
address the meeting:

John G. Winter, Esq.of Georgia

Rev. Wm. Carter of Tennessee, and

Gen. Prentiss of Illinois, late a

prisoner in the hands of the Rebels

Rev. E.U. Augbry of Mississippi

This announcement was signed by the following men:

Philip Fraser, Florida   J. L. Hathaway,

N.Carolina

J. C. Clapp, Florida

W. A. Guryer,
N. Carolina

J. L. Sammis, Florida

N. K. Jones,
N. Carolina

Calvin L. Robinson,
Florida

J. G. Winslow,
N. Carolina

William Alsop, Florida

John Diath [?],
N. Carolina

L. D. Stickney, Florida

John G. Winter,
N. Carolina

Paran Moody, Florida

James Mattoir,
Georgia

E. F. Parker, Florida

J. N. Bird,
S. Carolina

Joseph Remington,
Florida

Walter S. Carr,
S. Carolina

J. S. Duggs, Florida

N. T. Campbell,
Tennessee

C. N. Blood, Florida

Abbot Smith,
Tennessee

E. C. Howe, Florida

A. Bosseranan,
Virginia

And *one hundred others*

On that Saturday night, October 25, 1862, Cooper Institute was crowded almost to suffocation by what was said to be one of the most intelligent audiences of New York City. A full report of this meeting appeared in the newspapers the next morning. That in the New York *Tribune* ran as follows, to wit:

SLAVEHOLDERS FOR EMANICIPATION

MASS MEETING AT COOPER INSTITUTE

Speeches by Hon. A.J. Hamilton of Texas, Rev. W.B. Carter of Tennessee, T.J. Boynton of Florida, Rev. Mr. Augbry of Mississippi, and Horace Greeley.

Exiles from the southern States now in this city, compelled to flee from their homes for their fidelity to the Union, Held a Mass Meeting on Saturday morning in the large hall of the Cooper Institute to express their views generally on the Rebellion and the way to put it down. The importance of the meeting, an expression of the Union sentiment of the South now forcibly repressed in the Rebel States by the halter, the bullet, the cauldron, and the stake, attracted a much larger audience than the vast hall could accommodate.

A very large number of distinguished gentlemen of the city as well as of the South, included the Mayor, Charles King, and George Bancroft were on the platform.

The following resolutions, which had previously been adopted by the Union citizens of the South, were then read and presented by C.L Robinson.

The President then said that they had come there to listen to the voices of those who had suffered. They would listen to reasons why the resolutions should pass before a vote would be taken on them. (Applause) He then introduced the Hon. A.J. Hamilton of Texas who was rapturously applauded—the audience rising, waving hats, and giving rousing cheers.

After Judge Hamilton, several other southern Loyalists addressed the meeting, all of whom roused the greatest enthusiasm, and were constantly cheered. The resolutions were then unanimously adopted.

Horace Greeley, having come upon the platform and being discovered by the audience, was loudly called for, and he spoke briefly but very emphatically, and he closed the meeting, offering the following resolution, to wit:

That the thanks of this meeting be tendered to the Union martyrs and heroes from the south, who have addressed us tonight, with the assurance that their cause is our cause, and that the arms of the Republic shall never be grounded until justice is done for them and upon their enemies.

His Resolution was unanimously adopted and the meeting adjourned.

For some two weeks after this meeting, the Union loyalists were many of them greatly sought after to address ward clubs and large gatherings in different parts of the city and its suburbs.

I spoke one night at the Republican Club Room in the 17th Ward, the next at Steuben Hall with Horace Greeley, the next at Green Point with Col. S. L. Woodford, and night following with Rev. Dr. Cox and Hon. Lyman Tremain to an immense gathering in the Brooklyn Academy of Music. These meetings were held in the interest of the Union and a vigorous prosecution of the war, as against Copperheadism and Rebellion in the campaign of 1862, that memorable struggle between Wadsworth and Seymour for the governorship of New York state.

XV

SECOND UNION OCCUPATION

My Return to Florida

December 1862

$\mathcal{O}$n the 6$^\text{th}$ of December, I left New York with the Florida Tax Commission for Hilton Head. They stopped some ten days at Hilton Head and reached Fernandina, Florida, about the 20$^\text{th}$ day of December, 1862. They immediately commenced the work of their mission by establishing an office there and took steps to assess the tax upon that city and Amelia Island, which were then under the full control of the Federal troops.

The Commission's work moved forward quite slowly, however, and there being other assistants and desiring more active exercise, I soon discontinued my connection with the Commission, and commenced a small business at merchandising in the city of Fernandina. I purchased of the military governor, General Saxton, a remnant of a stock which had been abandoned and left by some retreating Rebel sympathizer when the town had been occupied by the Union forces.

The Second Occupation of Jacksonville

Early in the March following [1863] an expedition was organized at Hilton Head and sent down to the possession of Jacksonville, reaching that place on March 7th. The troops were composed of part of the 6th Connecticut Regiment, the whole of the 8th Maine under Colonel Guss, and the 34th Colored Troops under the famous Colonel Montgomery of Kansas notoriety. The city was not occupied by any force of Confederates except a picket guard, and the Union troops landed without opposition and took possession of the town.

What the object of this occupation of Jacksonville, at this time was, I never have been able to learn or seen anyone who knew. It seems not to have been intended to be permanent, for in four weeks it was again evacuated apparently without any object or excuse, the same as it was taken. While President Lincoln had promised and proposed, no doubt, to retake the town, to hold it permanently, we have reason to believe he knew nothing of this moment till after it was again evacuated. It seems to have been a freak of General Hunter's, perhaps for the exercise of his troops.

Jacksonville's east side of Ocean Street near Bay Street c. 1864
showing Union soldiers and their rifles
From collections at the Jacksonville Historical Society Archives

At all events, after they had held the town about one month, the place was again abandoned. Many Union people who had not an opportunity or did not choose to leave at the first evacuation, now accompanied the Union troops and went north or remained at Fernandina or St. Augustine.

At this time General Saxton was acting as military governor of the states of South Carolina, Georgia, and Florida, or of whatever portions of those states were or should be under the control of the U.S. troops. This duty was to relieve the Military Department of the care of the refugees and noncombatants, white or black, to provide for their employment, superintendence and education, and to take charge of all abandoned or captured property. Colonel J.M. Latta was appointed provost marshal of the state of Florida by General Saxton, and was charged with the duties of his office in the state.

When this expedition set out for Florida, Colonel Latta commissioned me as his deputy and directed that I should take possession of abandoned property found by the U.S. forces in Jacksonville. The following is a copy of the order of Colonel Latta. [This order, dated Fernandina, Fla., March 13, 1863, and the following one, dated Beaufort, S.C., March 13, 1863, have been lost.]

In pursuance of this authority, I proceeded to Jacksonville on the 14th of March and entered on the duties assigned me. On the approval of the Federal troops, many families who sympathized with the Confederate cause and were living there hurriedly left again, most of them leaving nearly all their household goods in their dwellings. The approach of the forces to the city was so sudden that they had no time to move them.

In the discharge of my duty, I took an inventory of all these articles and kept a full account of them in a book prepared for that purpose. Some of these articles of furniture were requested by the officers to furnish their quarters. These I furnished, taking the officers' receipts for the same. Not only household goods, but all articles of merchandise and produce found or captured were turned over to me and taken charge of by soldiers detailed for my service.

One day, word came to me that a company of Irish soldiers belonging to the 8th Maine Regiment encamped near the Catholic Church, had broken into and were pillaging the church. I immediately took a file of soldiers and went to the spot. I found that not only the church, but also the priest's residence adjoining the church, had been rifled by those Irishmen, and pictures, relics, and furniture had been carried to their camps.

I instituted a search in their quarters, and found these articles hid away in their tents. Even bedding and mattresses had been taken. All articles found were taken back, and a guard placed over the church and dwelling.

It seemed a strange thing to me that these Catholic Irishmen could bring their consciences to allow them or that they could find it in their hearts to steal from dwellings and churches and from the very altars and sanctuaries. I asked one man who had taken a picture of the Holy Mother how he could do it. He replied, "Somebody else would steal it if I don't, and I would rather have it than that some heathen should get it." They were very much enraged on being compelled to give up these articles, and threatened to burn the property.

And sure enough, the next day they set fire to the church at midday. Going to the spot immediately upon hearing the alarm, I found these Catholic Irishmen about in the streets among the crowd, with the pipes of the old church organ in their hands, blowing them and making the day hideous with their discordant noises. This is the history of the destruction of the old Catholic Church.

Colonel Guss, commander of this regiment, was in command of the post, and I hazard the assertion that a more inefficient officer and a more ruffianly regiment was not in the service. During this occupation, the Rebel troops gathered in considerable numbers outside of the town. Once or twice the Union forces marched out and tried to engage them or flank them. But they retreated up the railroad by which means they had approached the town.

The City Shelled

At other times when the enemy was reported near the city, the gunboats lying in the river by the town opened fire, sending heavy shell over the town after them. Not to be outdone altogether in this heavy artillery practice, the Rebels procured a heavy Blakely rifled gun from Savannah. They came down one night within three miles of town on the railroad with the gun on a platform car, and sent over into the town some half a dozen heavy, long six-inch rifle shells into the very heart of the city in the dead hour of night. One or two of them burst just before striking, but most of them did not burst.

One of these missiles exploded over the west end of the St. James Park. The butt of the shell, made of wrought iron, fell in the street in front of where the Windsor Hotel now stands. Another piece from the body or cast iron portion struck the old Academy building which stood where now stands the Park Theatre, about four feet from the side on the west end, passing inwardly and down through the floor within two feet of Dr. J.D. Mitchell's head as he was sleeping on a cot. He was the surgeon of the 8th Maine Regiment at that time.

Another fragment struck the balustrade on the upper piazza of Dr. Webster's residence on Monroe Street. Still another tore through the venetian blind on the front of Major I.D. Hart's old residence, which stood where Caulk's Stable now stands. A shell that did not burst passed through the residence of Paran Moody, the same he now occupies, entering in the gable on the west end and passing through the house and out the east end about six feet from the ground and buried itself some five feet in the garden.

Another unexploded shell passed over the roof of my house and through a little bakery building on the lot now occupied by the residence of Rivas and Koopman. Another passed through a two-story brick building, built by Major I.D. Hart and used as his office, which stands on the northwest corner of Pine and Adams Streets.

XVI

JACKSONVILLE'S
SECOND BURNING

After an occupation of about four weeks, an order came from headquarters at Hilton Head that the troops return to that point. The next day the second evacuation of our town took place. Soldiers are generally expected to have no opinion or preference about their movements, but to go as they are moved sometimes into pleasant quarters and sunny places, and again, to those disagreeable and dismal.

But the 8th Maine Regiment and the larger half of the 6th Connecticut, which garrisoned Jacksonville on this occasion, not only had an opinion of the "childs' play" movement they were enacting, but also they exhibited in an emphatic manner their

Members of the Union's artillery pose before their Jacksonville encampment.
(Note the soldier with a pipe in his mouth playing with the small dog).
From collections at the Jacksonville Historical Society Archives

disgust for the policy of "marching up the hill and then marching down again" by firing the town before they left it. They were,
moreover, comfortably quartered in abandoned houses and in a
pleasant climate, and they disliked to "pull up stakes" so soon
and return to their old quarters.

One fire was set by soldiers of the 8th Maine, who were
quartered in the dwelling of Thomas Ludwith, standing where
the mansion of his son William now stands. Another fire was set
by the 6th Connecticut, quartered in the mansion of Judge
Pierson, which stood on the lot south of the present residence of
Dr. Kenworth—this fire burned the Episcopal Church. The
third fire was kindled by a mulatto soldier named Isaac Smith of
Colonel Montgomery's regiment, and this fire burned in the second story of Bisbee and Canova's brick store, which occupied the
spot now covered by Hazeltine's block.

Each of these fires was kindled with the straw and moss
that the men had used for their bedding and were set on fire as
they left their quarters. The wind was quite strong, blowing
southwest. The fire of Bisbee and Canova's store communicated
with Dr. Baldwin's office and residence and moved on in a north-
easterly direction, laying in ashes a wide belt through the middle
of the town. The destruction would have been much greater
except that a heavy rain set in.[14]

It had been asserted by some that this burning was done in
retaliation for the wanton destruction of my property and the
Judson House block by the Confederate mob the year before. But

this was not the motive of those who set these fires. It was done by privates who were strangers to Jacksonville, who could not have known the facts concerning the previous burning of the town.

Of the property in my hands, the furniture was all left—most of it in the houses where it was found. Produce, cotton, sugar, etc., was carried away with us and turned over to the officer in charge at Hilton Head. I then returned to Fernandina and resumed my business there on the fourth or fifth of April, 1863.[15]

XVII

THE SORRY
PICTURE OF MY
FINANCES

*D*uring the previous summer in 1862, while I was in the East, I visited Boston, where my creditors—the merchants from whom I purchased goods before the commencement of the war—resided and to whom I was indebted at that time for some $41,000.

I made a report to these creditors concerning my business and what had befallen me in a statement of my assets after the war broke out:

Assets at beginning of hostilities:

$125,000

Debt I owed:

$ 41,000

Stock of goods destroyed:

46,000

Lumber and interest in the mill burned:

30,000

Store and warehouse burnt:

5,000

Debts due me by the people of Florida:

$40,000

Southern bank bills I saved:

12,000

And my store lots,

value unknown ?

Left and remaining at this time, claims for

goods sold:

$40,000

A sorry picture, indeed.

They told me that they approved entirely of the course I had taken, that they hoped I would collect what could be collected out of the wreck after the war, and if I ever got in a position to make them a proposition for a settlement of their claims, I might do so, but that they should never trouble me.

Back in Florida, Fall 1863

During the autumn of 1863, previous to my return south,

I learned that the tax commissioners were about to begin operations in Florida. My creditors had written me that if I would attend these sales and could bid on some of this property which would probably sell very low, they would take this property off my hands after the war and pay me the old assessed valuation as it had before the war. These monies would then be used to pay off my debt to them.

With this object in view, I attended these sales and bid on a large number of lots, paying for them out of the proceeds of the bank bills from the buried wine bottles which I had received from 55 cents to 65 cents on the dollar. It will be readily perceived that these lots must have sold *very low* from the very circumstances of the case.

At the time of this sale it was the darkest hour of our war with Rebels. There were but few buyers at the place, and they, with very little money. The strong doubt existed in the minds of everyone at the sale that the North would ever succeed in conquering the rebellion. All bidders were unwilling to pay out "good money" on so "bad a chance." The lots sold very low.

At the close of the war I conveyed to those northern creditors of mine, property which was assessed before the war at $24,300, and they credited me with that amount. It cost me $1,825. This was the reason why I bought so large an amount of the lots sold at the tax sale. I subsequently paid my creditors 50 cents on the dollar on the balance of my debt, and they gave me receipts showing it paid in full.

XVIII

THE SUFFERING OF
THE COLORED PEOPLE

*D*uring the Spring of 1863, there was a good deal of suffering among the colored people, who had, from the time the place was taken by the Union forces, been constantly coming through the lines to Fernandina, to the number of over fifteen hundred.

Removed from the restraints of their Rebel owners and not compelled to regular habits of eating, sleeping, etc., these ignorant people slept crowded into the close plastered rooms of abandoned Rebel houses. They ate just as it happened, but mostly

Jacksonville's Bay and Ocean Streets under Union occupation

From collections at the Jacksonville Historical Society Archives

after nightfall, and gorged themselves, and having little exercise as there was no work for them to do, large numbers of them became sick.

There was no physician available except the military surgeon at the posts, and he did not have the time nor inclination to attend to these people. Being familiar with the usual treatment of all the common complaints of the latitude, I was able to assist the people in visiting the sick and prescribing for them. It was good to be able to help them.

General Saxton appointed me to be the superintendent of the schools which were soon established to educate the colored people, both in day schools and in Sunday schools. My appointment to take charge of the Sabbath schools gave great offense to the Rev. Mr. Kennedy, a missionary of the Scotch Presbyterian Church, as he had been sent out from somewhere in Pennsylvania to labor among these people.

My care of the day schools also was a great affliction to one H.H. Hulpers, who had been sent to take charge of the "contrabands," as they were called, to see that they were provided with quarters, to deal out provisions to such as needed, and to assist them to employment as far as it was possible. He claimed that the care of their education came within his province.

The colored people, however, were not well pleased with the ministrations of this Hulpers, and they came to me to help them in various ways, and particularly to purchase lots at the U.S. tax sale. Quite a number of them who had been able to get a little money from employment in the quartermaster's service came to me, and I bid in cheap lots for them, as the lots were selling very low indeed.

This was claimed to be a decided interference with the duties of the superintendent, and he was quite angry with me and set himself to making up charges against me of a want of fairness and speculation in these purchases at the expense of the colored men.

These charges he sent on to General Saxton, and a copy of them was sent to me. I succeeded in satisfying the general very soon that I was not guilty of any of these charges or of any unfairness towards the colored men. On the contrary, they proved that I had been the friend of the colored man under all circumstances.

The following is a copy of the letter of Colonel H.M. Plaisted, then in command of the island, whose statement should have more weight, perhaps, than that of any other person at the post. I have letters of a number of the officers and teachers employed at this post equally strong. Colonel Plaisted has since been a candidate for governor of the state of Maine.

Headquarters 1st Brigade

Morris Island, S.C.

January 26, 1864

Hon. J. J. Lewis

Com. Int. Rev.

Washington, D.C.

Dear Sir:

I am requested to address to you a communication stating that I know of the transactions of C.L. Robinson with the colored men at the tax sales last summer, and of the charges Mr. Hulpers made against him in relation to these transactions.

I was commandant of that post at the time of the tax sale referred to, and for several months I had good opportunities for knowing the nature of those charges; for every colored man who thought himself aggrieved, applied to me as post commander for their redress.

I am happy to say that no case was brought to my knowledge which in the least reflected upon Mr. Robinson's character for honesty or fair dealing or in any manner upon his character as a friend of the colored man. He was accused of making the colored men pay more for their lands than paid at the sales.

These charges had this foundation: The form of the offer was: "The Government bids tax, penalty, and costs, who bids more?" "Twenty dollars," says Mr. Robinson, bidding for the colored man, and the Negro hears it struck off to him at that figure and upon hearing to pay thir-

ty dollars instead of twenty, he is astonished and
. . . *made to believe* he has been cheated, though
the difference is "Tax, penalty, and costs."

Then Mr. Robinson was accused of refusing
to let the colored men have their lands after he
had bought them. I presume that every com-
plaint of that kind came before me, and every
one upon examination resulted as follows: "Did
you furnish Mr. Robinson the money to buy the
lot for you?" " No." "Did he promise to buy it
for you?" "No." "Did you expect him to buy it
for you?" "No."

In my judgment Mr. Robinson did more for
the colored folks at those sales than any other
white man—more than all the others besides. If
he was not a friend of the colored man, a friend
in need and at all times, I know of no one who
was.

I firmly believe he was their true friend, and
in all his dealings with them, just and honorable.

I have the honor to be, sir,

Your most obedient servant,

H.M. Plaisted

Col. 11th Maine Volunteers

Comdg. 1st Brigade

I mention these things here because some of my Rebel friends (?) have within a few years reported that I was guilty of cheating the colored people during the war and that charges were preferred against me. This was the only instance in which charges were made during the war or that I was ever accused of wrong or unfairness to anyone.

Establishment of an Orphanage

At the above-mentioned tax sales, at the suggestion of Miss Chloe Merrick, the leading teacher of the colored schools, I bought a large mansion, the former residence of General Joseph E. Finnegan at Fernandina, for an asylum for the fatherless and motherless colored children. There were many such children within the Union lines, drifting about, sometimes suffering for want of care.

The object of this noble and faithful Christian woman in the establishment of this institution was to take up these waifs of colored humanity from the low associations and neglect from which they suffered and quite literally, while they were being educated, to give them a better general and social education as well.

The one great drawback to the immediate advancement of the freedmen, which could be expected from giving them only a common short education, was the vicious association in their home life with their ignorant and depraved slave parents and neighbors. By this home training which the organization would be able to give them through having the whole care of these children, friends of this enterprise believed that they could raise up a class of high order of teachers, preachers, fathers and mothers who in turn would become instructors and leaders of these people.

Having purchased the building, we had to furnish it and provide for its support. To effect this, Miss Merrick and I went to New York on July 23 of that summer (1863) and presented the claims of this enterprise to the Freedman's Aid Society of that city, as well as to well-known and prominent philanthropists. Our efforts met with marked success, and furnishings were procured for our colored orphan asylum as well as the means to support it from this time on.

XIX

RECOVERY

*A*fter this objective was assured, I went to Vermont and spent the remainder of the summer and most of the autumn with my family and friends.

Late in November [1863], I returned again to Fernandina. I found the orphan asylum already in working order and prospering. Miss Merrick was in charge with a corps of assistants and nearly fifty orphan children from two to fourteen years of age under her care.

The tax commissioners returned to Fernandina about the 10th of December and proceeded to St. Augustine. On December 21, they sold property which had been assessed there early in the summer and advertised for unpaid taxes. I attended this sale and bought for my wife a half-dozen fine lots with buildings upon them. These properties began paying rent almost from the day of their purchase.

Clerk of the Court

Soon after this, Judge Fraser organized the United States District Court at St. Augustine, and he appointed me clerk of his court. From this time till the first of February [1864], I was there attending to my duties as clerk and to my small business of merchandising at Fernandina.

Early after our arrival at St. Augustine, a meeting was held of the loyalists of that old city and of the many from Jacksonville and Fernandina together with a large number of refugees from the Rebel conscription going on in the interior of Florida. Strong resolutions were passed which denounced the Confederate usurpation and favored the national authority while urging the organization at an early date of the state authority by the local citizens.

Having succeeded in liquidating almost all my outside debts by selling my real property plus considerable amounts belonging to my wife, I then conveyed to her, as an act of simple justice in her repayment, several other pieces of property. This I did through her sister—about all I had, except the house we lived in. But by this means I was now able to repay her for more than half the means of hers that I had used in paying my debts.

While I am relating the acts of persecution visited upon me after the war, I should not forget to mention that I had been so unfortunate as to be subpoenaed by the government as a witness in some of the Confederate cases just before the close of the war. My testimony to the facts within my knowledge I could not under oath conceal. Being of record and coming to the knowledge of some of the old Rebel owners of the property condemned, the southern hostility towards me knew no bounds.

One of these men who had, as a member of the secession convention, been the father of the ordinance of secession, on seeing the testimony as true, swore a great oath that he would crush that d———d Robinson. And he ever after acted on that pledge.

He was an attorney-at-law, and he induced a number of planters in the interior to bring suit against me. These planters had sold to a cotton speculator large lots of cotton, mostly on credit, and had lost heavily by that speculator when the price of cotton went down.

I had acted as factor and forwarding merchant for the speculator. The said attorney assured the planters that with the juries we were having in the courts at that time, he could make me pay for every pound of that cotton, alleging that I was the principal in these operations and that the speculator was only MY agent!

This was indeed an effective persecution. With the juries of old Rebels that we were having before the reconstruction, the chance for my being saddled with judgments for the whole of these debts was inevitable.

POSTSCRIPT

[handwritten in pencil, apparently after the war years]

Some people seem to have been born to good luck, and others are forever followed by misfortune. Whether the fault is in them or in their "stars" it is perhaps not easy to tell.

While I would not be classed as an extreme case, probably in either direction, it does seem that I have had to contend with fully my share of "unpropitious circumstances," over most of which I could reasonably be said to have no control.

In the first place, on account of several very severe illnesses in my childhood, I have ever been of very slender constitution, in fact much of an invalid all my life. While this has very often stood in the way of my success, yet being hopeful and ambitious, I have never given up to any infirmity, but have led a very active life in spite of them.

I set out in early life to obtain a liberal education, but I was compelled from ill health to abandon my college course in the junior year. This was a great disappointment, but it was partially made up to me in a few years afterward by the receipt from my alma mater (the University of Vermont) of the honorary degree of Master of Arts.

Notwithstanding my inability to pursue further my academic course, I did not at once abandon the pursuit which I had chosen for a life work—that of teaching, but I continue to follow it, and with most satisfactory success, until a failure of health under the confinement of this, my chosen profession, compelled me to leave this most delightful of all occupations and seek a more active and open-air employment. I soon after engaged in the wholesale mercantile business in the city of Boston.

This I followed only four years, when on account of the rigor of the climate of that city, I was constrained to seek a milder latitude, and I took up my residence in Florida in December, 1857. In this delightful climate I was blessed with much better health. In September, 1858, I engaged in a large merchandising business in the city of Jacksonville, Florida.

This I continued with remarkable success until the breaking out of the war in the beginning of 1861, and indeed for over a year afterwards, as far as the disturbed conditions of society there would permit, till early in March, 1862.

At that time, while I had taken but little part in the prevailing excitement, being an invalid and a noncombatant, I had purposed to stand aloof from any participation in the contest going on. I had from the beginning decidedly opposed the secession movement. The Confederates pronounced me an enemy to the country, and on March 11, 1862, they drove me from my home, pillaged my goods, and burned my store as well as my sawmill and a large quantity of lumber, amounting in all to over $80,000 dollars, putting me in debt to my northern creditors for more than $40,000.

For three years my family were homeless, but were cared for by our Vermont friends. In February, 1864, the Union forces having taken possession of Jacksonville, I again began merchandising at that place, with very little to go upon except a good credit.

I prospered and made money again, but afterwards, in compromising and settling those ante-war debts, I reduced my business capital to a very low ebb. Soon after this came the great downfall in the prices of cotton, and I lost very heavily in this article, having at the time a large quantity on hand. All kinds of goods soon depreciated in value, and I soon after found that I was again stranded in business.

Other troubles by this time began to present themselves. While the repentant Rebels were coming back to their old homes after the war, they were apparently very friendly to me, and, having at this time a large influence with the military authorities, I was constantly being importuned by these returning Confederates to use my influence with the officers in control of affairs in assisting them to readjust themselves in their old homes and find something to do for a livelihood. This was no small tax on my time and charity, but in no instance did I refuse my serv-ices when requested in this behalf.

But this condition of dependence on the part of the Rebels did not last long. The military governor of Florida under President Johnson's policy made rapid haste to place all power and control of local affairs in the hands of those returned Rebels. These men were not long in waxing independent and they "kicked." They showed their real hatred against everything that was Federal and particularly against all that had been Union in sentiment and had not, like themselves and the fox in the fable, "lost their tails in the trap."

These men, who had been so smiling and polite to me when I was strong to assist them with the military, now were cold in their deportment and would only stiffly notice me in the streets. And this state of feeling has changed very little up to this day.

It is true that at times, when business intercourse for a while identified our interests, we would become more familiar. Then I would flatter myself with certain ones among them, that the old hostility had now entirely subsided. But it would not be long before something would occur to show me that I was mis-taken. The same old hostility was indeed still there and was only latent for the time. Having been more prominent in my Unionism, I was now the more prominent object of this hostili-ty and their secret persecution.

This persecution came to interfere seriously in my busi-ness, and it was the prime cause why I could not proceed. No

southern man patronized me in trade or in anything he could
buy from a southern man or even from a less radical Unionist.

These instances have been innumerable. When in doing
business with or for persons—perhaps some simple-hearted
negro—he has said that one or another of these prominent
Rebels had told him "not to patronize Robinson" or "not to trust
his business to Robinson, for he was not worth of confidence."
This has been a continuous thing ever since the return of the first
Rebels after Lee's surrender.

And all this time these persons, when squarely confronted
and questioned by my friends as to what there was against
Robinson, have produced nothing substantial. At most, the
charges were that Robinson purchased the property of the "dear
southern people" during the war when it had been confiscated or
up for tax sales. The Rebels said Robinson would not surrender the
property to them when they came back after the war was over.

To this latter charge, I plead guilty. I would explain that I
had been impoverished through the war spirit and that these
owners contributed their best to inflame in the destruction of
nearly all my property. The little remaining had been confiscated
and bought up by these same people during the war. Therefore,
I considered it only the perfection of justice that I should make
up at least a portion of my losses out of purchases at confiscation
sales held by the United States government.

But, nevertheless, at the close of the war, be it remembered
I sold back to these old owners or bought their quit claim to

every piece of this property. Yet I have reason to believe that this in no instant ever diminished that secret hostility.

I can in no other way account for the magnitude and persistence of this opposition and spite. Let me say that I have ever sought by strict attention "to mind my own business" and by careful and upright personal conduct to all people to disarm this spiteful sentiment.

The southern people were ever clannish. They hang together in cliques, and against the northern people they are as one man. Formerly and even now there are districts where few northern people are settled. Society arranges itself under a certain leading man or family: Colonel somebody or Judge somebody leads each faction.

Between them and their adherents, there is a constant variance, a latent state of war, and the type of the contest, whether it manifests itself in open hostility or in a suppressed variance and opposition, depends on the intelligence and civilization of the people. It is the province of the leaders whether or not it appears in open outbreak or in a more quiet partnership, and the fact is the same: it is always there. It seems to have been a natural outgrowth of the habit of domination peculiar to the prevailing institutions of the country.

Whether Jones or Smith is a good reliable man or not, in the mind of the person you consult as to his character and standing, depends altogether upon the fact whether Jones or Smith belong to our clan or party or not. If he is one of *our* party and sides with us, he is a "perfectly reliable gentleman." If he be a friend of the other party, he is a "damned rascal."

This thing has always prevailed in the South to an astonishing degree. And now when northern people, in any numbers, are settled among them, their old clan distinctions become less marked among themselves, but they cling to a man against the Yankees.

This is not at first apparent to the newcomer. They are usually smiling and polite to him at first, but when he is settled down among them, he soon finds that he has no rights that they feel bound to respect, especially as against a southern man. No Ku Klux Klan organization is needed among them for this purpose. It is generally understood and the universal feeling which exists from the very habit and training (or lack of training) under the shadow of slavery.

The result of this condition of things is that when a northern man becomes obnoxious to one of these people, he is obnoxious to all. If he hits or offends one, he offends all, and all proscribe him and openly or secretly are against him and consider it their duty to punish him.

It is *not so* among the northern settlers in the South or anywhere else. These men were brought up in society where every man stands on his own merit and looks out for himself. One's enemies would not dare to lie about him in northern society, for if he does, it is sure to recoil on themselves. The standard of truthfulness is higher, and common honesty is much more generally inculcated from the cradle to the grave.

As things now exist in the South, the Southerners hang together, and defend and help each other right or wrong. The Northerners are "every one for himself and the D——l take the hindmost."

As long as the new settler bows and bends and never ruffles his southern neighbor (and they are overbearing from their early habits and training from youth up), he may get along smoothly. But woe to him who asserts his independence and offends one of these dear people. He can never again conciliate them.

As for me, my offense was a radical one. It was a notorious one. I had been a Unionist during the war, but I was a Republican after its close. I had bought some of the dear people's property at a confiscation sale. I had favored negro suffrage and cast my vote for it as a delegate at the great southern loyalist convention in 1866.

Also, I had, as U.S. commissioner, issued warrants for the arrest of Ku Klux Klan members and held them for trial. These were sins past all forgiveness. Nearly the whole body of southern people in Florida are unanimous in their hostility and opposition and are ready to pronounce me "bad." They have vilified me from first to last in every way they dared to do it—when not openly, by whispering and innuendoes. My courage has been such, as a citizen and neighbor, as to afford the least material for slanderers to lay hold upon me. In their denunciations, they don't give particulars. But this matters but little. They all denounce you generally and insist that what many say must be true.

Items are not necessary. If the whole southern people say a man is "bad," that they consider sufficient: he must be "bad." If you ask for particulars, they consider it sufficient to put more emphasis on the "bad."

This opposition damaged my merchandising and prevented my rising again when I was crippled by heavy losses in cotton and the resulting depreciation in goods on hand. It hung like a dark cloud over my real estate agency business and, like a heavy weight, dragged down the earliest and grandest efforts that were made to extend abroad a knowledge of (and build up the resources of) Florida, thus preventing my making that business a support to my family.

In 1869, finding I could not continue my merchandising on account of the business debt my losses had left on my shoulders, I began to close out my concerns and pay up those debts. I had to resort to real estate sales to accomplish this. I sold not only what real estate I could on my own, but also what real estate my wife had consented to sell from her holdings. She also gave me her rent monies to pay up these debts.

I had still many notes and accounts against various citizens, mostly southern, both from before the war and after. But these debtors insisted that I should be indulgent and wait upon them as they were just then rising out of the ashes of the war. It would not do for me to push these demands. Their hostility was too pronounced already.

I expected, however, to realize on these claims eventually, and with the proceeds to pay up my wife the money of hers I had used. But in 1869, the legislature passed a Homestead Exemption Act, which rendered nearly all my demands uncollectable. This and the new U.S. bankruptcy law made me poor indeed. But, rather than avail myself of the provisions of the Bankruptcy Act, I resolved to pay up my wife by conveying to her the real estate I had not been able to sell. And as I needed no capital for the business of real estate brokerage, which I was now building up, I would save the reputation of becoming a voluntary Bankrupt. I thought I could make a living still.

EPILOGUE

Calvin L. Robinson died on July 4, 1887. That year the following eulogy was published in a book by C.A. Rohrabacher entitled *Live Towns and Progressive Men of Florida*:

> Amongst Jacksonville's most cultured and honored citizens stands forth prominent the Hon. Calvin L. Robinson, a gentleman who has carved out a career which will live with the history of the State. . . . [He] was appointed Provost Marshal under General Lawton, then Military Governor of the State. Later...he engaged in real estate, and two years after added the practice of law. . . . He also organized and is President of the

Marion Land and Improvement Company. . . .
Mr. Robinson was in great measure responsible
for the building of the beautifully located town
of Belleview. . . . [He] is the owner of the
Drysdale addition to Jacksonville. . . . For twen-
ty-eight years he has been a member of Solomon
Lodge of Free Masons: he was one of the organ-
izers of Duval Division, Sons of Temperance, in
1869, and was the architect and builder of the
Trinity M.E. Church, of which he has always
been President of the Board of Trustees. . . .

It is through men such as this, possessing
wealth and moral influence, that Florida has
been brought to her present state of prosperity,
and in such hands her future progress may be
looked upon as assured.[16]

Appendix

LETTER FROM ELIZABETH ROBINSON

This letter was written by Robinson's wife, Elizabeth, to her sister, who then sent it to a newspaper in Boston for publication.

From the *Boston Journal*, March 30, 1862

The Sufferings of Unionists at the South

The following touching letter from a lady in Jacksonville, a native of New England, illustrates the brutality and oppressive tyranny of the rebels. It is to be hoped that those who have been released from this galling tyranny, by the success of our arms, will be fully protected by the Government, and that wherever the flag is planted by the advancing army of the Union, the protection will be permanently maintained. A temporary occupation of any Southern city would cruelly compromise many noble men and women who, like the writer of this letter, have remained true to their allegiance.

Jacksonville, March 17, 1862

My Dear Sister:

The Yankees have at last come and brought joy to our poor hearts. They came in time to save our lives, but not our property from these merciless Southerners; for last Tuesday night, they burnt Calvin's store and warehouse to the ground and hunted for him to shoot him. They would point their guns at the store windows, fire and wish that "this might hit him," but through the mercy of God, his life was preserved. I know you will be interested in all the particulars, dear sister, and I will try and write them.

In the first place they call every person born north of Mason and Dixon's line by the meanest name they can command. With the confederates or secessionists, "Yankee" is meaner than "nigger," the lowest name a person can have. Until the Federalists came, there was in our very midst a company of desperadoes calling themselves Guerrillas, whose avowed intention was to destroy the property and kill every northern man, particularly Unionists, and now they are lurking about the country so that we do not really feel safe.

O, I wish we were in dear old New England. Calvin and Polly [Polly was the family nickname for loyal Ivanowski, a Pole] have never done anything to provoke the people, but a great many seemed to annoy them. They have a great many friends now, but they are overpowered and stand in fear of these guerrillas. Several months ago, Calvin and Polly thought it would be a good plan to send part of their goods to Savannah and get good money, for the money here is "no account." Certain men stopped them, declaring they should do no such thing. At the commencement of this trouble ten days ago, all the merchants sent off their goods in the greatest panic by rail into the country to be lost by the way or stolen. They were very angry because we would not do the same.

A week ago tonight, I do not think there was more than a dozen families left in town, and most of these are too poor to leave.

Even the Presbyterian minister told a widow and her child if they did not leave the place, they were as bad as the rest. They were "Yankees" and they ought to go into the woods and live, even if there was danger of starving, rather than remain among such a people. Everyone tried to get away on the cars, and people tell us that crowds of women and children are camping out in the woods along the line of the railroad between here and Lake City, a distance of about sixty miles. And it is true that a *great* many suffer for food.

The past week has been a perfect reign of terror—such sights and sounds I pray my Heavenly Father I may never see or hear again, or any of those I love. If I did not sincerely believe that not a sparrow falleth to the ground without our Father's notice, and that He careth for the least of us, I should wish to die. This trouble has nearly broken our hearts. To think that people who have so long professed such friendship for us, and for whom we have done so much, became such bitter enemies without any cause unless it was that we would not destroy our property ourselves and run into the woods because "the Federals were coming." We thought we knew who were our friends, but I do think that many were so ignorant as to suppose they should all be destroyed when the Federal soldiers came.

For a long time there had been a great many threats in circulation that Jacksonville was to be "wiped out and become the battle field"—that they would commence at each extremity of the town and drive out the "nest of Yankees"—and all imaginable threats; and we daily watched and prayed for deliverance to come. Our kind

Father saw fit to send it just as He did, and we will not dare to question His providence.

We expected the fleet a week ago yesterday (Sunday), but it did not come until Wednesday following, the next morning after the store was destroyed. That very night of the fire, Calvin and Polly thought it best to take the children and myself and go first across the river to a neighbor's, who had left town the night before, and succeeded in finding a vacant house there.

There had been a rumor that day that an armed body of men were coming, some said to burn the town, others thought only the mills and foundry. I could not believe the story, but was willing to do as they thought best.

While on our way to the store, before we went across the river, we came right upon these men, about five hundred, all armed with guns, and it is a wonder they did not stop Calvin for he had his shawl on his arm. He heard someone in the ranks utter his name with an oath.

It was a terrible time. Like fugitives we *fled from home* with our babies and just a blanket apiece. We started in a drenching rain, the wind blowing a perfect gale. As we left the wharf I feared it was the last time I should see the store. My fears were realized, for only the walls remain. The wharf and warehouse are entirely destroyed, except for a few boards, from which we stepped into the boat.

These soldiers came on the cars, but blew no whistle to warn people, and then marched through the streets as quietly as possible. They were in town about an hour when they fired the foundry at the lower part of the town, next the mills, one after another. One mill was very near us where we stayed. Men were lurking around the house all night. I think there were seven mills. We stood nearly all night where we could watch the progress of the fires. We saw the torches pass up and down the river among the mills, and finally stop at the end of the warehouse. Immediately the end was in flames.

At the same time, we heard several guns, one after another; they were firing at Mr. Parker and the clerk, a noble young man. I did not imagine anything so horrible at the time, but Calvin did, and we were in the greatest anxiety for Mr. Parker's safety. He could not go over the river with us, for he "could not think they would trouble the store, but if they should, he was alone and could take care of himself."

It seems they escaped in a boat, (Mr. Parker and the clerk), and as they left the wharf, they fired ten or twelve times at them, very near indeed, but Mr. Parker laid flat in the boat. As they could not see him, they said they had shot him. Mr. Ivanowski, the clerk, paddled the boat across the river (about one mile wide) with a shingle, and then they separated.

Mr. Parker wandered in the woods twenty-seven hours in the rain, without food, afraid of his enemies, unacquainted with the country, but at last he reached St. Augustine. During this time three men on horseback, *friends,* were searching for him but did not succeed in finding him. The clerk found him about four o'clock the next morning. He is now home at St. Augustine.

I cannot tell you half the misery of that night; we have not recovered from the effects yet. It was passing from one extreme of *sorrow* to ecstasy of *joy* when we saw the *fleet coming up the river.* When the vessels got in front of our hiding place, we rushed down to the landing with a sheet, and soon had a flag waving, and what with crying and laughing, we made a funny figure. I cried for joy once in my life, and since now, I cannot contain my feelings when I think of their timely arrival.

Calvin jumped into his boat and went aboard one of the vessels, rowed to town and returned at night, giving a glowing description of his reception. We remained one night more over the river, then spent one in a warehouse near the gunboats, and the remainder at home. We have not been able to sleep much or rest for there have been so many rumors afloat of an attack here, and I have so many fears for dear Calvin's safety that I can take no comfort. We will put our trust in the Lord and pray He will deliver us from our enemies.

Do remember us in our trouble, dear Carrie.

Your loving sister, Lizzie

[Elizabeth Seymour Robinson, Calvin's wife]

Notes

1. Robinson was born in Reading, Vermont, on June 3, 1828.

2. Martin, *Jacksonville's Ordeal by Fire*, p. 32: "By 1860, Robinson was one of the leading merchants in town and owned most of the waterfront block on the south side of Bay Street between Hogan and Laura streets. Robinson's major enterprise, a large two-story wholesale and retail store, stood at the southeast corner of Hogan and Bay streets, with the rear opening onto a wharf, where he operated a large warehouse, two hundred feet in length. To the east stood another two-level store owned by Robinson, which adjoined his lumber yard and planning mills, where he cut lumber to order and sold various equipment and supplies for sawmills. Farther east was yet another Robinson enterprise—a tin shop and a retail outlet for stoves, hollow ware and tin ware. Robinson also operated a steam sawmill on the waterfront. . . . at the foot of Catherine Street."

3. Martin, p. 32: "The war had escalated rapidly from the time of Fort Sumter's surrender on April 13, 1861. Two days later, Abraham Lincoln began mobilizing the North, calling for the enlistment of 75,000 three-month volunteers. On April 19, the U.S. Navy launched a blockage of Southern ports along the Atlantic and Gulf coasts, and on May 6, the Confederate Congress responded to these acts with a declaration, 'recognizing the existence of war between the United States and the Confederate States.'"

4. Martin, p. 52: "The schism in the city's population became more pronounced, feelings grew more bitter, and a 'brutal element of ruffianism', directed against known Unionists, began to surface. Threats were made on the lives of Robinson and other Northern merchants, open harassment and denunciations on streets and in stores increased, and surreptitious attempts to extort money from Unionist families in exchange for their safety, were made by the more unscrupulous vigilantes."

5. Hanna, *Florida, Land of Change*, p. 275: "Financing the government during this war tested all the skill and ingenuity of the state. . . . In the course of the struggle other currencies arose. There were Confederate notes, usually considered less valuable than those of the state. Also railroads and corporations issued notes of small denomination, and certain cities followed suit. . . . The state debt of Florida for the period she was out of the Union consisted of $2,450,000 in treasury notes and $500,000 in bonds. On the collapse of the Confederacy in 1865, $1,800,000 in notes were in circulation and $300,000 in bonds."

6. Martin, p. 66: "On the evening of March 8, a small expeditionary force, consisting of four gunboats, two armed steamers, six armed launches and several cutters, and a transport carrying eight companies of the 4th New Hampshire, arrived off the mouth of the St. Johns. There they would be held up for three days attempting to cross over the treacherous bar, but within

moments of being sighted news of their arrival was flashed to Jacksonville over a telegraph line that had been rigged up for this purpose between the city and Mayport Mills."

7. Martin, p. 71: "With the departure of many of the city's older and more influential Southern residents, Jacksonville's Unionists, most of them Northern merchants, were left to the mercies of a mob that was beginning to range with increasing belligerence and hysteria through the city streets. Calvin Robinson was warned by friends that a plan was afoot to murder him and destroy his property. Also singled out for execution was Robinson's closest friend, attorney Philip Fraser, a forty-two-year-old Pennsylvanian who had lived in Jacksonville since 1841, and had served as mayor in 1855."

8. Hanna, p. 285: "The net gain of this first invasion was Fernandina and St. Augustine which passed permanently into Union hands. Jacksonville was evacuated within a week. This was disastrous for her, because during the following year she was occupied twice by federal troops: once in October, 1862, and again in March, 1863. Both attacks were hardly more than raids, resulting in little beside wanton destruction."

9. For further details of the Unionists' meetings, see Martin, pp. 81-83.

10. Davis, p. 251: "The day after the first interview with General Sherman a meeting was held in the public square of Jacksonville. About 100 Unionists were present. Resolutions were adopted which protested against the abrogation of the United States

authority and proclaimed the ordinance of secession 'null and void' because it had never been submitted to the votes of the people."

11. Martin, p. 88: "About fifty of the Jacksonville refugees, among them the Robinsons, Frasers, and Keenes, eventually boarded the transport *Star of the South* for New York City, where they were greeted as heroes. In a special appearance before the New York City Council, Mayor George Opkyke described (them) as destitute fugitives. . . . "

12. *New York Evening Post,* unknown date.

13 Robinson's father, Louis Robinson, lived his whole life in South Reading, Vermont, until his death in 1871.

14. About six blocks were burned out, and more than 25 buildings were destroyed. See Martin, p.132.

15. Martin, pp. 245-46: "When Colonel Higginson and the U.S. Colored Troop regiments occupied Jacksonville in March 1863, Robinson was with them, looking into the possibility of starting up in the town once again. When the forces were withdrawn, Robinson made his way to Fernandina and concentrated on his merchandising business."

16. Rohrabacher, *Live Towns and Progressive Men of Florida,* pp. 80-82.

Selected Bibliography

A Committee Publication: Florida Civil War Centennial Committee and Florida.

Burnett, Gene M. *Florida's Past,* vol. 2. Sarasota, FL: Pineapple Press, 1988.

Davis, T. Frederick. *History of Jacksonville, Florida and Vicinity, 1513 to 1924.* Gainesville, FL: University of Florida Press, 1964.

Davis, William W. *The Civil War and Reconstruction in Florida.* New York, NY: Longmans, Green, 1913.

Dovell, J.E. *Florida: Historic, Dramatic, Contemporary,* vol. 2. New York, NY: Lewis Historical Publishing, 1952.

Foster, John T., and Sarah W. Foster. "The Transformation of Florida," in *Beechers, Stowes, and Yankee Strangers.* Gainesville, FL: University Press of Florida, 1999.

Hanna, Kathryn A. *Florida, Land of Change.* 2nd ed. Chapel Hill, NC: University of North Carolina Press, 1948.

Library and Historical Commission. *Florida, a Hundred Years Ago.* Tallahassee, FL: State Library of Florida, 1966.

Martin, Richard A., with Daniel L. Schafer. *Jacksonville's Ordeal by Fire.* Jacksonville, FL: Florida Publishing Company, 1984.

Rohrabacher, C.A. *Live Towns and Progressive Men of Florida.* Jacksonville, FL: Times-Union Printing & Publishing House, 1887.

Shofner, Jerrell H. "Reconstruction and Renewal, 1865-1877," in Michael Gannon, ed., *The New History of Florida.* Gainesville, FL: University Press of Florida, 1996.

Tebeau, Charlton W. *A History of Florida.* Coral Gables, FL: University of Miami Press, 1971.

If you enjoyed reading this book, here are some other books from Pineapple Press on related topics. For a complete catalog, write to Pineapple Press, P.O. Box 3889, Sarasota, FL 34230 or call 1-800-PINEAPL (746-3275). Or visit our website at www.pineapplepress.com.

Discovering the Civil War in Florida by Paul Taylor. The Civil War in Florida may not have been the scene for decisive battles everyone remembers, but Florida played her part. From Marianna and Tallahassee in northwest Florida to Fort Myers and Key West in the south, this book covers the land and sea skirmishes that made Florida a bloody battleground for four sad years. ISBN 1-56164-234-7 (hb); ISBN 1-56164- 235-5 (pb)

At the Edge of Honor, the nationally acclaimed naval Civil War novel by Robert Macomber, takes the reader into the steamy world of Key West and the Caribbean in 1863. Peter Wake, a reluctant New England volunteer officer, finds himself battling the enemy on the coasts of Florida, sinister intrigue in Spanish Havana and the British Bahamas, and social taboos in Key West when he falls in love with the daughter of a Confederate zealot. ISBN 1-56164- 252-5 (hb)

Point of Honor, sequel to *At the Edge of Honor,* by Robert Macomber. Peter Wake is in command of a larger ship and beginning offensive operations on the Florida coast during the tumultuous year of 1864. Along the way he hunts down army deserters on uninhabited islands, risks international confrontation on a sea chase to French waters, and makes the most momentous decision of his personal life. ISBN 1-56164- 270-3 (hb)

Confederate Money by Paul Varnes. Two young men from Florida set out on an adventure during the Civil War to exchange $25,000 in Confederate dollars for silver that will hold its value if the Union wins. Training to be physicians, they get mixed up in some of the war's bloodiest battles, including the largest battle fought in Florida, at Olustee. Along the way, they meet historical characters like Generals Grant and Lee, tangle with criminals, become heroes, and fall in love. ISBN 1-56164- 271-1 (hb)

200 Quick Looks at Florida History by James Clark. Florida has a long and complex history, but few of us have time to read it in depth. So here are 200 quick looks at Florida's 10,000 years of history from the arrival of the first natives to the present, packed with unusual and little-known facts and stories. ISBN 1-56164- 200-2 (pb)

Florida Portrait by Jerrell Shofner. Packed with hundreds of photos, this word-and-picture album traces the history of Florida from the Paleo-Indians to the rampant growth of the late twentieth century. ISBN 1-56164-121-9 (pb)